It's Never Too Late To Dance!

Finding The Joy In Ministry
(And In Yourself)

Donald H. Neidigk

CSS Publishing Company, Inc.

Lima, Ohio

IT'S NEVER TOO LATE TO DANCE

FIRST EDITION
Copyright © 2023
by CSS Publishing Co., Inc.

Library of Congress Cataloging-in-Publication Data
Names: Neidigk, Donald, 1949- author.
Title: It's never too late to dance : dance steps to joy in ministry to
  self / Donald H. Neidigk.
Description: First edition. | Lima, Ohio : CSS Publishing Company, Inc.,
  2022.
Identifiers: LCCN 2022001484 (print) | LCCN 2022001485 (ebook) | ISBN
  9780788030420 | ISBN 9780788030437 (ebook)
Subjects: LCSH: Joy--Religious aspects--Christianity. |
  Happiness--Religious aspects--Christianity. | Dance--Religious
  aspects--Christianity.
Classification: LCC BV4647.J68 N45 2022 (print) | LCC BV4647.J68 (ebook)
  | DDC 246/.7--dc23/eng/20220216
LC record available at https://lccn.loc.gov/2022001484
LC ebook record available at https://lccn.loc.gov/2022001485

For more information about CSS Publishing Company resources, visit our website at www.csspub.com, email us at csr@csspub.com, or call (800) 241-4056.

e-book:
ISBN-13: 978-0-7880-3043-7
ISBN-10: 0-7880-3043-4

ISBN-13: 978-0-7880-3042-0
ISBN-10: 0-7880-3042-6

PRINTED IN USA

Table Of Contents

Foreword

This book was written partly as a "note to self" after experiencing a major tragedy in my life, the death of my daughter-in-law, April, in December of 2015. In the aftermath, I felt despair and heartbreak such as I'd never known before. Then, after this little book was completed, my grandson Mikey was diagnosed with leukemia when he was just two years old and, after a three-year-long fight, is now in heaven.

For three years the focus of life for my wife Kathy and me was helping with Mikey's care and assisting my son and his new wife in their struggle against this childhood killer. After chemotherapy, two bone marrow transplants, and radiation, our little superhero lost his earthly battle but now soars with the angels.

Often, I have wondered where God was in all this. At times, I've thought I should retire from the pulpit since a purpose of ministry is to inspire hope through the gospel, and I wasn't feeling very hopeful. But remaining in ministry, even in times of my own sorrow and agony, pointing others to Jesus can be a powerful object lesson for those who are hurting — both fellow church workers and people in the pew.

Regaining and maintaining joy in the midst of grief and emotional exhaustion is why I have put these thoughts down, both for myself and for those who minister to others. It is my experience that the dance steps to joy in this book, when there is determination to practice them, actually helps one remain on the dance floor of life and ministry.

In all honesty, I admit that my personal faith has been shaken and I've had frequent moments of doubt and unbelief in the past five years. But as I intentionally practice these dance steps, I find myself healing and transitioning to more frequent moments of joy.

Moreover, I find it supremely reassuring that despite my own bouts of unbelief, God still believes in me. I'm still on the dance floor because his son Jesus carried me there, and now holds my hand whether in the shadow of death or in the sunshine of life.

If there is any monetary gain to me from the sale of *It's Never Too Late To Dance: Dance Steps To Joy In Ministry To Self,* it will be used to help families who have a child in treatment for pediatric cancer.

Soli Deo Gloria!

Preface

"Oh, excuse me," I said for the second time to the petite middle-aged lady with short dark hair and glasses I was in danger of tripping over in the hotel breakfast buffet line. She just smiled and moved deftly out of the way once more.

The dining room that morning at the Elegante Hotel and Resort was full of police officers and their spouses who had come to Ruidoso, New Mexico, for their annual spring convention. Just after Easter, my wife Kathy and I had booked a weekend there to recover from more than a year of caring for our son Nathan and his two small children after our daughter-in-law April had died. Kathy really needed a break, and some time to grieve.

"No problem!" the mystery lady said with a winning smile and west Texas accent that made her seem delightfully pretty. Then, moments later, I did it again! This time I backed into her and practically knocked her breakfast tray to the floor.

"You know, the dance was last night," I joked as we bobbed and weaved out of each other's way.

"Oh, it's never too late to dance!" she quipped, still smiling.

And that was the end of the encounter. But it made a lasting impression. All that day, and frequently since, I've thought about her quick and witty reply, *It's never too late to dance.* What an amazing approach to life!

It's never too late to dance, even in the breakfast buffet line when you're in danger of falling down and dumping your food everywhere. Even when you're grieving the death of a loved one, even when you're exhausted, and even when you're past middle age and entering your sunset years, it is never too late.

That evening, I made my usual phone call to my elderly mother, Rhoda, and told her about the incident. She's home bound and seldom gets out except for the occasional errand or trip to the doctor.

"Well, not everyone can dance," she told me, after I recounted the incident and repeated the lady's words. Then she added, "How can you dance when you have to use a walker?" "Mumsy," I answered, "I'm speaking metaphorically when I say it's never too late to dance. I'm saying there are ways we can think, choices we can make and actions we can take that can make our lives happier."

"Oh, if you put it that way, I guess it's so," she answered. "But I usually think of all the bad things."

"Exactly!" I answered. "And when you approach things that way, always looking on the bad side of things, you're not dancing. You can dance, even with a walker, if you intentionally change the way you think and the way you approach life every day." My mind began spinning with hard learned truths about how to have a happy life, or in the language of metaphor, how to dance every day.

I instantly thought of Audrey, the same age as my mother, whose circumstances were similar. Audrey would literally have to be in the hospital before she'd miss out on a dance or any other social activity. If there was a party at church or an exercise class at the senior center, or an installation service for a new pastor, she'd be there, even with her walker, wheelchair or oxygen tank. I've often joked with Audrey about how she's the oldest teenager I know. In her eighties she was still playing softball with our church youth on a mission trip to El Paso. Even in her wheelchair Audrey dances.

Being Lutheran, I can't help but consider how the *Small Catechism* of Dr. Martin Luther and his explanation of the Ten Commandments supports the idea of dancing every day. Though the commandments as Moses records them are mostly negative, Luther turns them upside down and makes them positive. Thus, when the commandment says, "You shall not give false testimony against your neighbor," Luther says it also means, "We should explain everything in the kindest possible way."

Usually when someone says or does something that looks bad, especially someone we don't particularly like, our natural impulse is to jump to the worst possible explanation for their behavior. This might give us a moment of *schadenfreude*, hurtful joy, as the Germans would say. But it doesn't make our day any happier. On the other hand, when we deliberately choose to explain the words or actions of another person in a positive way, our day can be much brighter.

After my encounter with the lady at the hotel, and with Luther's positive approach in mind, I began compiling a list of what I call *"Dance Steps To Joy."* I could have called them "Commandments for Joy," but people would instantly think I was writing about the law of Moses. I'm not.

Law keeping doesn't necessarily make anyone happy. About the best it can do is to keep us out of trouble. So, these are "Dance Steps To Joy," positive steps anyone can take to put some dancing — some joy — back in our lives.

Just to be clear, writing theology is not my purpose here. I can't help but do some of that — after all, I spent quite a few years of my life and lots of money at two graduate schools of theology, but that's not the main focus. Learning how to make informed choices that will leave our hearts dancing is really what these *Dance Steps To Joy* are all about.

One might think just having good theology would make us happy. It doesn't always. I know of one pastor whose theology was impeccable. He was always concerned that his fellow pastors be just as precise in their doctrinal formulation and church practice as he was. He was one of those people I call an "enforcer." When some of the pastors in my local pastors' conference didn't enforce the rules as he understood them, he refused to join us for Holy Communion. But clearly his strict approach to doctrine and practice didn't make him happy. He ended up having an affair, becoming estranged from his wife and eventually taking his own life. If he had only learned how to dance!

I'm assuming you've already sorted out your theological views. You're probably active in some form of ministry or human care. You probably aren't trying to "justify" yourself, that is, make yourself righteous, by obeying laws, rules and regulations. You trust Christ for your salvation. For those of us whose faith lies in Lutheran or reformed traditions, that's a given. But even if your beliefs don't reflect traditional Christian faith, I'm hopeful you'll find something here that applies to you.

Whoever you are, and whatever you believe, I'm pretty sure you'd like to experience more joy in your life. You'd like to dance again, or maybe even for the first time. And you can! That's the thesis here. *It's never too late to dance!* Wherever you are in your journey you can experience joy and dance with life.

I'm an example of one who realized in late middle age that feeling miserable, helpless, and victimized is a waste of time. Living each day at the mercy of controlling or negative people or waiting for random events to strike for good or evil is no way to enjoy life. I decided I needed to think and act in ways that were good and healthful for me, regardless of what anyone other than my wife thinks. I include her because we're a team. Her opinion matters.

"You have a right to breathe and take up space!" I frequently tell others. It's okay to be true to your own heart, to your own beliefs, values and priorities. In counseling, this is called *self-differentiation.* Unfortunately, though I've encouraged other people to live this way, and to do so assertively, I haven't always applied it to myself. But I'm done with that. Life's too short to live one's life according to anyone's conscience but one's own.

Martin Luther is often quoted as having said, "To go against conscience is neither right nor safe. Here I stand. God help me. I can do no other." (Different sources word it differently.) If that kind of personal integrity was good enough for Luther, it's good enough for me, I concluded. Once I decided that it was true for me, that I had the right to live according to what I believed to be right and good, I felt liberated. My feet got happy; I put my dancing shoes on.

One event in particular stands out as helping me rearrange my thinking. I was visiting with Helga, a member of my congregation, as she and others were exiting the worship service one Sunday morning. She was a really busy professional lady, so after the customary exchange of pleasantries about her job and her family she hurried toward the door. But as she backed against it and turned to leave, she got in the last word. *"Make* it a great day," she said.

10

"What a profound concept!" I said to myself as I watched Helga walk toward her car. Most people would say something, "Have a great day." But that's just a meaningless platitude, a polite wishful thought. It's like saying, "I hope a great day will just fall out of the sky and happen for you." But Helga was telling me that if I am to have a great day, I have to do something to make it so. It wasn't just going to fall out of the sky. *I* have to make it great myself. It's my responsibility to think and choose and act in ways that turn it into a great day. I am the actor, not merely the one acted upon.

That being true, I began to realize there is much I can do to promote my own happiness regardless of my circumstances. No matter how negative people are, or how unfairly I'm treated, or how badly things are going for me in life, I can think positively about myself and do things that are good for me. I can live as a free person whose worth, dignity, and joy are not tied up in someone else's beliefs, or their opinions of me, or their plans for my time and energy.

Pastors, and probably many others in the human care professions, tend to think their first duty in life is to see that everyone around them is happy and fulfilled, even if it means they must sacrifice or neglect themselves. But this is a recipe for resentment and misery. It's good to be concerned about the well-being of others, but self-care has to be a priority. If I'm happy and dancing with life as I serve others, it's more likely others will be happy and dancing too. But even so, I can't personally make anyone happy. Others are responsible for creating their own happiness.

Dr. William Glasser is one of my favorite counseling theorists. I highly recommend his famous book, *Choice Theory*. Dr. Glasser has much to say about creating our own happiness through the choices we make. One of the questions Dr. Glasser asks when he works with couples who come to him for marriage counseling is, "What are you willing to do this week to improve your marriage?" [1]

---

1 William Glasser, *Choice Theory: A New Psychology of Personal Freedom* (New York: Harper Perennial, a Division of HarperCollins Publishers, 1998) pp. 179-180.

Rather than waste hours and weeks of counseling time going over what a couple thinks is wrong with their marriage, Dr. Glasser zeros in on what they can do to improve their relationship. He takes a positive approach right from the start. Before couples even leave the room after their first session, they have to come up with commitments they will carry out to improve their marriage in the coming week.

This same positive approach can help anyone get back on the dance floor. Married or not, the same question, with minor modifications, works for anyone who's sick of being miserable and wants to take some responsibility for their own happiness. Ask yourself, "What can I do today to improve my life?"

And then start listing a few things. Keep it simple, things you can actually do today that will give you joy. I'd had my nose stuck to the grindstone of over-commitment and being super responsible for so long, I'd almost forgotten how to have some spontaneous fun. But I've learned I can still do it, I have a right to do it, and it doesn't have cost much of anything.

It's been years since I've had a vegetable garden. I've always been too busy. But lately I've been thinking, "It would be really fun to plant some tomatoes this year. I wonder if they still have mail order seed catalogs."

Well, barely had I started reconsidering the possibility of gardening when I noticed a castoff seed catalog on the counter at the post office, just begging me to take it home. I did, and I spent a marvelous hour in dreamland, paging through stunning pictures and descriptions of plants and trees. For a few bucks I could order some tomato seeds that promise to produce four-pound beauties! For a bit more money, I could order a miniature citrus tree that grows limes, tangerines, oranges, and lemons all on the same plant!

I was dancing as I studied that castoff seed catalog. You can be dancing too as soon as you determine it's okay for you to do something right now to improve your life. I have just one word of caution: Murphy's law says that if something can go wrong, it will. And often it does. With that in mind, after you decide what that enjoyable, simple, cheap, and easy-to-pull-off thing you're going to do to improve your life today is, have Plan B in mind. The devil, the Grinch, or whatever you want to call him, doesn't want God's children to be happy. The last thing in the world he wants is for you to "make it a great day" and "improve your life." Therefore, have a Plan B in mind, and maybe even a Plan C.

Here's how it works: Suppose you decide that having a picnic with a friend will set your heart to dancing today. (Half the fun is in the anticipation and preparation.) So, you pack your lunch basket, throw in a blanket, and head for the park. But about the time you get in the car, the weather turns sharply windy and cold. It's spitting rain. You can't go after all. Going to the park is now out of the question, but you still have Plan B in your pocket.

Plan B might be to spread out your lunch on a card table on the back porch under a protective roof and eat your potato salad and fried chicken while you and your friend watch the rain come down. If that's not possible, Plan C might be to cover the living room floor with your blanket and eat lunch there. And instead of throwing the frisbee, you might play checkers or a few hands of cards.

The point is — you can always come up with a plan to improve your life and dance. I have in my cupboard a coffee cup decorated with a Beatrix Potter style smiling rabbit and this inscription: "Bread and water can so easily become tea and toast." What will you turn into tea and toast today? What commitment will you make to yourself today to get your heart and feet dancing?

For about a year, I facilitated a support group for survivors of suicide loss. Unless you've experienced the loss of a loved one to suicide, it's impossible to realize the grief, suffering, and destruction a friend or relative who takes their own life leaves behind. I call it grief on steroids. All grief hurts terribly; I know from experience. My father died from cancer, my sister was murdered and my daughter-in-law ended her own life. Suicide loss was the worst grief I'd ever felt until my five-year-old grandson died from leukemia.

Although everyone in our support group had experienced the indescribable agony of suicide loss, at the end of each meeting, every participant was asked to share a "spark," something that gave them joy since the last meeting. You might think it impossible for anyone in a group like this to come up with something good that had happened to them, but almost everyone could.

A spark can be a few minutes of joy spent holding a grandbaby, or eating lunch out with a friend, or seeing a great movie, or finding the first zucchini in the garden. The possibilities are endless. The point is that no matter how bad our circumstances, there's always something good to celebrate.

And because of that, between the meetings, regular participants in the group actually looked for moments of joy in their lives they could share with others when they came to the next meeting. They looked for that spark and they found it. On their own, they fanned it into a flame of joy that left their hearts dancing. Then when they returned to the group and shared their spark, the other survivors smiled and were encouraged.

"What am I willing to do this week to improve my life?" Asking ourselves this question helps us realize there's always something we can do to improve our situation and create our own happiness. I can still be a rose, even if the room is full of onions. I don't have to wait for the onions to decide they want to smell better. So just what is it that I can do today to make my life happier, to put a skip in my step, to put me on the dance floor of life?

You can *choose* to dance today! It doesn't matter how old you are or how far along you are in your career. It doesn't matter if you're sick, or alone, or grieving, or poor, or whatever your situation. It's simply not true that "Old dogs can't learn new tricks." Of course they can! You can start thinking and behaving in new and positive ways anytime you want. As that wonderful lady said, *"It's never too late to dance."*

Dance Steps — Questions For Reflection

1. Would you describe yourself as being basically happy or unhappy? What do you think is most responsible for this: disposition, events, or choices you make?
2. Who is the happiest person you know? Why do you suppose this person is happy?
3. How has grief affected your life? What are you doing to cope with your pain and restore joy?
4. Has being so happy you felt like dancing ever made you feel guilty? Why?
5. What makes you worthy of joy? Do you think you have a right to rejoice and dance? Why or why not?
6. Do you agree that you must always make someone else happy before you can be happy? Why or why not?
7. Describe some of your happiest moments in life. What happy moments do you look forward to? What happy moments will probably never take place? What will you replace them with?
8. What role does faith play in your personal happiness? Or does it?
9. Is the idea of God a joy maker or joy breaker for you? Why?
10. What spark of joy did you experience recently that made your heart dance?
11. If you are stuck in life and not dancing, what can you do today to make yourself happier?

Does God Dance?

"It was fitting to celebrate and be glad, for this your brother was dead, and is alive; he was lost, and is found." Luke 15:32

In seminary, we used to joke about a mythical "St. Vinegar's Church." I've visited a few St. Vinegar's over the years. Maybe you attend a St. Vinegar's. Some churches seem to think it's sinful to be happy. Pietism may be partly responsible. Beginning in the 1600s, many Protestants became strongly influenced by Pietism. Pietism was a reaction against a stuffy Christian orthodoxy that didn't seem to offer a sense of the presence of God or feel a personal accountability to him. But 400 years later, Pietism hasn't necessarily been the antidote to sweeten up many of those St. Vinegar's churches that are still around.

In my view, Pietism overreacted when it concluded that having fun, enjoying life, playing sports or card games, going to the theater, or dancing were temptations of the devil. The English Puritans are an example of this, as well as some modern fundamentalist groups.

When I was in high school in the late 1960s, a girl named Linda declined my invitation to attend the prom with her. She said, "I wouldn't want to be found on the dance floor if Jesus should come." An elderly lady told me that as late as the early 1920s young people in her church youth group weren't allowed to dance. A retired pastor said that in the 1940s students at his seminary weren't allowed to get engaged until they had graduated and received their first call to a congregation. Even so, it was amazing that so many graduates married the day after they graduated. What fast courtships those must have been!

There was a rhyme kids used to say when I was little that reflected this outlook on the Christian life, "Quaker meeting has begun. No more laughing, no more fun. If you show your teeth or tongue, you shall pay a forfeit." My sisters and I would play the game and see how long we could keep from giggling. The first one who giggled lost.

Some of our older church music incorporates this dour outlook on the Christian life, especially in the tunes. I love the sturdy doctrinal content of reformation era hymns, but honestly, some of them sound like funeral dirges. Like, "In peace and joy I now depart, since God so wills it." We sang that song once in church when my middle son Nathan was a small boy. It made him cry.

Is a joyless faith what God wants us to experience? I don't think so, because it doesn't reflect the joy of God. God, whose chief attribute is love, and who loves to forgive, rejoices in his creation! He celebrates within himself and with all the angels and saints in heaven when a lost soul comes home.

So, does God dance? I would say, yes, absolutely God dances! Maybe he doesn't dance literally, but he definitely does metaphorically. There is so much in the Bible that depicts God's people celebrating the events of life with music, rejoicing, and even dancing. So, why would it be inappropriate to imagine God himself as dancing?

Consider the psalms. They're full of joyful hymns in which the creation praises God. "The heavens declare the glory of God, and the sky above proclaims his handiwork…. In them he has set a tent for the sun, which comes out like a bridegroom leaving his chamber, and, like a strong man, runs its course with joy." (Psalm 19:1, 4b-5) Can't you just see in your mind's eye the heavens dancing and singing as they praise God, and the sun popping up in the morning like a bridegroom leaping from his tent for joy?

Another psalm echoes this joy, "Let the rivers clap their hands; let the hills sing for joy together before the Lord." (Psalm 98:8-9b) Dancing, clapping, singing — this is God's intent for his creation. Not only is it his intent, it's uncontainable! All of creation was designed to leap and dance and sing and praise God. The fact of creation's existence is a sacred song and dance of praise.

Now, I never actually saw a river clap its hands, or a hill sing, or the sun leap like a happy bridegroom. These are metaphors. But human beings do clap, sing, and leap literally as expressions of joy. Where did our uncontainable desire to dance, sing, and rejoice come from?

Does God Dance?

I believe it reflects the original image of God in which he made us. One of the reasons we value, respect, and honor every human being is because we're told in Genesis that we were made in God's image. Yes, all of humanity is fallen; the Bible teaches us that. And from personal experience, we recognize we are all sinners. Even so, every person still bears something of our maker's image. Original holiness is gone unless it is restored through baptism and faith in Christ, but human nature nonetheless still reflects the Creator's image, though that reflection is far from perfect.

Therefore, when I honor and respect others, highborn or low, sick or well, strong or weak, old or young, whatever their race, culture or religion, I honor and respect God. Because of this divine imprint that every human being on the planet shares, Christian or not, tarnished by sin though we may be, all of us are worthy and sacred beings.

Moreover, to be made in the likeness of God means that the attributes of our nature are like his. In seminary, I learned that our abilities to reason, create, communicate, love, act justly, and practice mercy all come from the one in whose image we are made. All our highest aspirations come from the nature of God stamped on our being.

But there's more to us that reflects God's image that we don't hear much about in seminary or anywhere else for that matter. What about our universal feelings of sadness and joy? What about our inclinations toward weeping and laughter? What about longing and jealousy? *What about singing and dancing?* Where did all that come from? I believe these are all a reflection of the image of God in us as well.

That's why we see creation singing and clapping in the Psalms. That's why we see Miriam, the sister of Moses, dancing and playing her tambourine after Israel escapes slavery in Egypt. That's why we see the prophets describing the restoration of the nation with rejoicing and dancing and feasting. That's our nature. And it comes from God's nature.

What portrays that nature of God better than the story of the prodigal son? In the story, a young man asked his father for his inheritance early. So, the father obligingly divided up the property between his younger son and the older one. The younger son went away to a far country. There he lived wildly, wasted his money on prostitutes, and ended up so hungry he was tempted to eat the pods he was feeding the pigs. What a humiliation for a Jewish boy from a good family!

In despair, he decided to return home to his father. He planned to ask his father to treat him not as a son, but as a hired hand. He had his speech memorized. But barely had he set foot on the property than his father saw him. The father ran to his son, he threw his arms around him, and commanded that the finest robe, ring, and sandals be brought for him. He ordered the fattened calf to be slaughtered and a feast to be held, because "this my son was dead, and is alive again; he was lost, and is found" (Luke 15:24).

The older son came home. He heard the music and saw the dancing. He was not happy about it. He complained to his father. He said, "I've served you faithfully. I obeyed your every command. And you never even barbecued a goat for me. But you gave a party for this son of yours who has wasted everything you gave him!"

What did the father say to this highly offended older brother? He said, "*It was fitting to celebrate and be glad, for this your brother was dead, and is alive; he was lost, and is found*" (Luke 15:32). Did you catch that? "It was fitting to celebrate and be glad."

Reflect for a moment on who each of the characters in the parable represents. The younger son — who's he? He's everyone who has ever wandered away from God but has returned home. The older brother; what about him? He's all the self-righteous people in the world who refuse to forgive a repentant sinner. With an attitude like that, you'd never get this older brother out on the dance floor of life. And who's the Father? He's God, whose image is perfectly reflected in Jesus Christ, who welcomes and forgives sinners and celebrates with dancing whenever one comes home. This parable of the prodigal son gives us permission to loosen up, to take off our tie, to let go of our constraints and rejoice in God's grace and forgiveness.

An African-American pastor was the guest preacher during

chapel one day at seminary. He gave a rousing sermon such as most of us were not accustomed to hearing, let alone write and deliver. Animated, excited, funny, serious, moving — all these words are descriptive of his style. Yet his largely white audience scarcely managed a smile. Hardly anyone said "Amen!", even when he invited us to.

About half-way into his sermon, he simply stopped. A few seconds later he said, "The Bible says the dead in Christ will rise first and y'all gonna be the first to go!" That did it. Most of us cracked up. When the laughter died down, we didn't have any trouble feeling what we were hearing.

So, does God dance? You bet he does! Through his own example he gives us permission. He dances over his creation. He dances over his people. He dances over every wayward child who comes home. He dances over you and me. And if God dances, so can we. Let the party begin! Even if you're showing up late, *it's never too late to dance*!

Dance Steps — Questions For Reflection

1. In your mind, how does God look and act? Would you include such words as joyful or stern, judgmental or forgiving, distant or close? Why?

2. If you are a church member, would you describe your congregation as a place of darkness and negativity or brightness and joy? What makes it that way?

3. In New Mexico, a popular Native American deity is Kokopelli, the flute player. Would a description of the biblical God dancing and playing the flute offend you or cause you to smile? Why?

4. What about you best reflects the image of God as you have come to understand him? What about you least reflects the image of God?

5. Who do you have the most trouble forgiving? Why? Would the father in the story of the prodigal son forgive this person or not? Why?

6. Consider your criteria for forgiving others. Is it greater or less than God's? Explain.

7. What would make you more likely to dance, forgiving or holding a grudge? Why?

8. Which character in the story of the prodigal son are you most like right now? When have you been like the others?

9. Describe the type of worship experience you would most like to have. Is correct doctrine or a happy heart most important to you? Is it possible to have both? Explain.

10. Would you rather be on a mountainside watching a sunrise or in church hearing a sermon? Which is more likely to leave your heart dancing? Why?

11. After considering scripture, especially the psalms, what do you think heaven is like? What do you hope heaven is not like?

The First Dance Step To Joy — Dance With Your Life Plan!

"Trust in the Lord with all your heart, and do not lean on your own understanding. In all your ways acknowledge him, and he will make straight your paths." Proverbs 3:5-6

"When you're up to your neck in alligators, it's hard to remember that your initial objective was to drain the swamp." I heard that line during a training class I attended years ago.

Boy, is it ever true! You graduate from seminary with stars in your eyes, fully intending to save the world. And then you get called to St. Vinegar's Church. There, the warring factions take a break from intramural combat just long enough to put you through the meat grinder. Your idealism destroyed, you begin to wonder if maybe God is calling you to insurance sales or hotel management.

It doesn't need to be that way. You don't need to dance with porcupines. It's really up to you to decide which balls you're going to catch, which ones you're going to drop, and which ones you're going to throw back. So how do you determine that? A life plan helped me. It can get you dancing again too.

A life plan assumes you've taken an honest look at yourself. You know who you are as a unique child of God. And you know your tremendous worth to God, no matter what anyone else thinks of you. After all, he made you, and as Ethel Waters said, "God don't make no junk."

Yes, sometimes we disappoint God. It's called sin. The Bible says sin is whatever is not of faith (Romans 14:29). Sin is what happens when we don't live up to God's expectations of us, or our own expectations of ourselves.

It's why we don't always feel like dancing. Even so, God still loves us. And he's always offering us a second chance to get it right. He's even willing to pay for our dancing lessons!

23

The greatest evidence for this of course is that Jesus died for us. "Greater love has no one than this," says Jesus, "that someone lay down his life for his friends" (John 15:13).

Friends of God, that's who we are! That means we are of tremendous value! Every one of us is a prince or a princess on the dance floor of life. Keep that in mind as you take inventory of your gifts, your interests, your limitations, and your dreams in putting together a plan for your life. Then, as simply as possible, write it down. Just a few sentences are all that are needed; it's not an essay. Then, once written, it becomes your very own mission statement, your personal life plan.

After I wrote my life plan, I thumb tacked it to the shelf over my computer where I could be reminded of it every day. Now, with my life plan memorized, I try to evaluate every influence and choice that comes my way. I dance with what I want to be part of my life. I let somebody else dance with the rest.

As I learn to stick more consistently with my life plan, as I let it help me filter out what's not for me, I find myself to be a happier person. I discover that I "Wag More and Bark Less", as a bumper sticker I saw puts it. This then, is the first dance step to joy: Dance with a life plan.

Is this selfish? Is this narcissistic? It is if your life plan is focused only on pleasing yourself and not also on seeking the good of others. Obviously, a truly Christian life plan is one that's informed and guided by God's word and church. The Bible has a great deal to say about the importance of loving one's neighbor. So somehow that needs to be included. Happy people are caring people. They dance with opportunities to love their neighbor.

The ways I love my neighbor may be different from yours. Even so, the core values we share are going to be much the same. They will, that is, if our values are formed by the same spring of life, the word of God. In loving my neighbor, I may choose to send a monthly check to support my local homeless shelter, Joy Junction. Or maybe I'll choose to help prepare and serve meals at Noon Day Ministries. A friend of mine, Jim, enjoys teaching a Bible study in Spanish at God Cares About You, a street mission. Maybe you'd like to visit a person in the hospital who has no family nearby. Or maybe you would choose to love your neighbor in ways that never occurred to me.

The Roman Catholic Archbishop of Santa Fe, through a representative, spoke to the New Mexico legislature about a "formed conscience."[2] A formed conscience is not one just created willy-nilly out of the smorgasbord of the world's values. Rather it grows from the seeds of truth found in the Bible and planted in our hearts though preaching and teaching. The resulting flower may be different but the roots are the same.

That's what needs to be reflected in a Christian life plan, a conscience formed by our identity as God's children and his will for us as revealed in his word. The most perfect revelation of this word is Jesus Christ, whom we believe speaks the very words of God (John 12:49).

The more we learn of the nature of God through our encounter with his son in scripture, the more our mind and conscience and desire reflect God's will for our lives. After time spent in reflection and prayer, with the Spirit's help, we write down in simple language what becomes our life plan. Then we let it guide us in all we think and do. As we follow it, we find we're happier people who dance better and more frequently.

I haven't always known this or appreciated it. Frankly, it's only recently that I've begun practicing what I'm preaching. I confess that for much of my adult life I was overcommitted. I tried to fix everyone's problems and make everyone happy. But in trying to be all things to all people, I wasn't much of anything to anybody. It was exhausting. And I found myself getting angry with God. I definitely wasn't dancing and I was depriving others of learning how to dance on their own. It's taken me a while to learn that you can't dance for someone else. You can only dance for yourself.

My first awareness of this began one day after a graduate counseling class. My fellow students had exited the room and I was dumping my problems onto the instructor, a former nun

2 Micaiah Bilger, "Archbishop on Lawmaker Who Voted Against Ban on Late-Term Abortions: Can't be Catholic and Pro-Abortion", *LifeNews.com*, March 7, 2017. https://www.lifenews.com/2017/03/07/archbishop-on-lawmaker-who-voted-against-ban-on-late-term-abortions-cant-be-catholic-and-pro-abortion/

named Gene. Gene listened patiently as I told her about all my responsibilities and commitments and how they conflicted with my family obligations and all the things I really wanted to do but couldn't. When I finally came up for air she said very directly, "That's quite a heavy burden you've chosen for yourself."

It hit me like a ton of bricks! I wasn't the victim of my problems. I had created them by choosing to burden myself with unnecessary commitments. I needed to get a backbone. I needed some nerve so I could say "No" when I didn't really want to be someone else's baggage handler. If I was committed to something I didn't want to be committed to, I needed to respect the real me, apologize, and just back out. In the future, I needed to be much more selective in deciding which balls I was going to catch and which ones I was going to throw back.

An assignment in that class was writing a personal life plan. That's where I got the idea. My life plan has gone through several revisions but that's okay. It is, after all one's own life plan and nobody else's. You can change it anytime you want.

Mine says, "As a valued child of God, my purpose in life is to be a good husband, father, and grandfather (I added grandfather after my grandkids were born), use my gifts and training as a pastor, teacher, and counselor to help others, write for publication and for my own personal enjoyment, enjoy my old car hobby, and take time to smell the roses."

I've pretty much followed that for the last decade or so. I've lost interest in old cars and gotten it back, so that phrase comes and goes. On the helping others part, I went overboard. I poured so much energy into helping others I exhausted myself and endangered my health. Gene's words, "That's quite a heavy burden you've chosen for yourself," are still resonating with me. Now I try to help others in ways that fit into my personal and family priorities. I say "No" more often.

How did I get so tangled up in everyone else's problems and burdens that I was hurting myself and my family? Well, part of it was misunderstanding what it is to be a caring person. Caring people want to help others. But helping others isn't necessarily doing their work for them, or relieving them of emotional pain, or saving them from failure, or eliminating their stress by taking their stress and discomfort upon oneself. That approach to caring is a recipe for self-destruction.

I can't tell you how much I looked forward to retirement because of the heavy burden I had chosen for myself. It would have been more conducive to my personal dancing if I had written into my life plan that "My role as a pastor, teacher, and counselor is to help others accept responsibility for their actions, learn from their failures and make better choices."

What I've needed, and perhaps what you need, is to get some nerve and backbone. Life plans only work when we determine to live by them, even when doing so means somebody else is going to be unhappy with us. For years, I continued trying to please everyone and of course if I pleased one, someone else was displeased.

Worrying about displeasing other people has meant lots of stomachaches and sleepless nights. My chaplain resident supervisor at Presbyterian Hospital, John, taught me to exercise some "pastoral authority," to exercise some nerve and go with what I know is right, even if that means unhappy people. If I make people unhappy, then oh well, there will be unhappy people. But at least I can live with my conscience, my stomachaches will go away, I'll sleep better and I'll feel a lot more like dancing.

I remember a slogan from the Vietnam era, "What if they gave a war and nobody came?" Just because somebody wants to fight doesn't mean we have to jump in the ring. Sometimes we can choose our battles. Sometimes we can choose our burdens. If a fight isn't part of your life plan, and you have a choice, just don't show up.

It's good to have a life plan, but keep in mind that despite our best plans, sometimes we have to modify them. Even God plans, and changes his plans. God, the Bible says, "declares the end from the beginning" (Isaiah 46:10). God perfectly knows his own mind. He knows his own nature. He knows all he intends to do and why. And according to Saint Paul, "all of God's plans are grounded in his love" (Ephesians 1:4).

But occasionally in the Bible we see God change his plans. He would warn through the prophets that he was about to punish his stubborn and idolatrous people. But when the people took to heart God's warning and mended their ways, what did God do? He changed his plans! "And the Lord relented from the disaster that he had spoken of bringing on his people," Moses tells us (Exodus 32:14). If God can have a plan and change it when he needs to, why can't we? I think we can.

"Do you know how to make God laugh? Make plans." That's what one of my sons texted me recently. I get it. No matter how perfect our plans may seem, unforeseen events happen and we end up tossing our plans right out the window. Stuff happens. Events take place that can upset everything. We can either brood about it, or we can make different plans. But they can still fit into our original life plan if we've written it well, acknowledging the role of God in our lives.

In my original life plan, I said my intention was to be a good husband, father, and grandfather. There was also an unwritten but mental clause that my wife and I would take a cross country train ride when we retired. Well, now we're retired but that clause was put on hold when we began helping raise two grandchildren almost fulltime. Shortly after that responsibility lessened, we accepted another one, helping with the care of a grandson with leukemia.

So, Kathy and I may not be taking a transcontinental train ride any time soon. But I think I'm doing a pretty good job being a husband, father, and grandfather. Upholding that part of my life plan means I still have something to dance about.

A life plan is all about finding meaning and achieving success as we are informed by the Bible and as we understand our unique selves. It's not something imposed on us by someone else, our parents, our spouse, our friends, or even trusted advisors. The life plan they think is best for us may not be. No one can deliver to me the right life plan but myself.

A life plan can help us be happy, but it doesn't guarantee success in everything I pursue. Maybe in my life plan I envision opening a business. So, I pour my talent and energy into it for years, but in the end the business doesn't make it. I go bankrupt. I grieve over my lost business.

Does that mean I'm a failure? Well, if my life plan defines success as building a profitable business, then yes, I'm a failure. But if my life plan defines success in terms of working hard, being honest, doing my best for the customer, and honoring God in all I do, then I'm a smashing success. Even if the business fails, I still have a reason to dance.

Years ago, I attended the retirement dinner put on by Mobil Petroleum Corporation for my Dad and his co-worker. Both men had worked hard and served the company faithfully for many years. Then at age 65, both retired. The dinner was held at the Hobbs, New Mexico, country club. It was a lovely banquet with appreciative speeches given by the supervisors. At the conclusion each man received a gift. My Dad got a set of luggage. The other man got a complete fishing outfit. Within a couple of weeks, the other man died of a heart attack. My Dad lived for another fifteen years.

What was the difference? I don't know this for a fact but I suspect that the identity, purpose, and self-worth of the man who died were inseparably connected to his job. Retirement was traumatic for him. He no longer had a reason to live. When his job ended, so did his life. On the other hand, my Dad was deeply involved in his church, he was constantly trying to keep his children connected to each other, he was always planning another building project for himself or for a neighbor, and he went out and found part time employment. His job at Mobil was only part of what gave him meaning. There was plenty more.

But life plans aren't just about "doing." They're about "being." A wise man, perhaps Deepak Chopra, (others have said it also) is quoted as saying "We are human beings, not human doings." With that in mind, at pastors' conferences I sometimes ask fellow clergy in private moments, "How are things going?"

Almost to a person, each pastor has started telling me about their church; whether the attendance is up or down, how the finances are, what the different groups are doing, new people that have joined, unhappy people that have left, and so on. It became clear to me that for most pastors, their personal sense of joy, success and value is inseparably connected to their job.

So, my concern for them is that if the job goes away, so will their sense of self-worth.

Now I ask different questions, like these: "What's been giving you joy lately?" "What are you doing to take care of yourself?" "Who has made a difference in your life?" Once or twice, I've sprung a question on a pastor that I picked up from a "Three Stooges" comedy. Curly, Joe, — or maybe it's Larry — knocks on the door. The snooty butler answers and asks, "Who are you?" Curly replies, "Fine. Who are you?"

Nobody expects to be asked, "Who are you?" We're not used to such a query in casual conversation. Spring it on a colleague sometime and watch the reaction. But whether you ask a colleague or not, each of us needs to ask that question or ourselves if we're to find out who we are and what it takes for us to dance. Then, as we gather answers, we can begin putting together our life plan; we can start filtering out some of the things that sidetrack us, and we can get on with what life can be about: dancing.

Where are you in life's journey? Do you know? Are you careening through life, like a pin ball in an arcade machine, or are you dancing to your personal life plan, a plan you've created for yourself? If you haven't written one yet, now is a great time to get started. It doesn't matter how old you are or where you are in your career. Since it's never too late to dance, you can take the first step any time.

Not long ago, I did a funeral for a man I didn't know. His pastor was out of town and as a friend of the funeral director I agreed to do the service. Before the service I met with the family; the widow, the sons, a daughter-in-law, and a granddaughter. As I spoke with them, I was trying to get a sense of who this man was.

What did I learn? I learned he served his country in the Air Force, that he took his sons to ball games, that he was a big Dallas Cowboys fan, and that he spent his entire working life balancing the weight of cargo in airplanes. Was he a success? I don't know. It depends entirely on what his personal definition of success was. If his life plan was that he would be a faithful husband, father, and worker, and enjoy his favorite sport, then he was a great success.

How will you measure your success? A pizza company has a commercial that asks, "What do you want on your Tombstone?" What they mean is, "Do you want pepperoni or extra cheese on your pizza?" But when we ask that of ourselves, we're concerned with how we want to be remembered. If you create your own life plan and then let it guide you, you can honestly have engraved on your tombstone the words from Frank Sinatra's song, "I did it my way," or for our purposes here, "I danced with my life plan."

Maybe it never occurred to you to write a life plan. Don't beat yourself up over it. If you're reading this, it's not too late. Today's a great day to come up with one, wherever you are in the journey. Get a piece of paper and a pencil, sit down, think it through, and write it out. Maybe, like me, you wish you'd done it decades ago. But it doesn't matter when you do it. As the Nike slogan says, "Just do it!" because it's never too late to dance.

Dance Steps — Questions For Reflection

1. What unforeseen events have distracted you from working toward and achieving personal goals?
2. If the cost of engraving wasn't an issue, what would you want written on your tombstone?
3. How does recognizing that you are a loved and valued child of God affect your plans and decisions?
4. What principles or virtues would you say best characterize you? How closely would this correspond to a friend or co-worker's evaluation of you?
5. What projects, causes, tasks, or interests excite your passion?
6. How are your passions and interests reflected in your life right now?
7. What would a perfect week look like for you? What would it include? What would it not include?
8. How does loving your neighbor show itself in a typical day for you?
9. What burdens have you chosen for yourself that don't really fit with your personal values, goals or interests?
10. If you could add something to your life that's missing, what would it be?
11. Take as much time as you need and write out for yourself a personal life plan. Then begin using your life plan to evaluate the choices and decisions you make every day. Feel free to edit and modify it as your interests and circumstances change. After all, it's your own personal life plan.

The Second Dance Step To Joy — Dance With Who You Are!

"I say to everyone among you not to think of himself more highly than he ought to think, but to think with sober judgment, each according to the measure of faith that God has assigned." Romans 12:3

I've always liked men's hats. The Men's Hat Store on Central Avenue in Albuquerque is one of my favorite places to visit. I'm about ready for a new straw Panama. Every so often I'll drop into the store, try on some hats and buy one. I usually know which one I want before I go in, but I'll still check out a derby, a Homburg, a top hat, or a red fedora and look in the mirror to see what I look like wearing it. It's always good for a laugh.

Why do I laugh? Because many of the hats look so silly on me. I'm not a derby, Homburg, or brightly colored fedora kind of guy. Just give me a black, dark gray, or brown fedora. The wider the brim, the better. Even though someone else might think a fedora looks silly on me, I still enjoy wearing one.

That comes from knowing who I am and being okay with who I am. No, it's more than that; it's being delighted with who I am. I'm kind of a geeky guy and I like geeky hats. That's the way God made me. In fact, because God made each us with the personality, the abilities, the talents, the physical features, the likes and dislikes we have, we can rejoice in our individuality. It all comes from him! And because it does, we can dance with who we are.

Saint Paul tells us not to think more highly of ourselves than we ought, but to evaluate ourselves with sober judgment (Romans 12:3). At first glance, that might sound like a put-down. It sounds like Paul could be saying, "Hey, buddy, who made you king of the world? You ought to be ashamed of yourself, breathing and taking up space like you do." But that's not what he's saying.

He's saying, do some sober self-reflection. Find out who you are and what special gifts you have from God. Then, be who you are and use your gifts joyfully. That's dancing!

I have to admit I've heard some sermons and sung some hymns that focus far more on what's wrong with me than what there is about me that's cause for dancing. I wonder if in school you had to read the famous sermon "Sinners in the Hands of an Angry God" like I did? Puritan preacher Jonathan Edwards wrote it in 1741. Here are just a few lines from the sermon:

The God that holds you over the pit of hell, much as one holds a spider, or some loathsome insect over the fire, abhors you, and is dreadfully provoked: his wrath towards you burns like fire; he looks upon you as worthy of nothing else, but to be cast into the fire; he is of purer eyes than to bear to have you in his sight; you are ten thousand times more abominable in his eyes, than the most hateful venomous serpent is in ours. [3]

It's a very long sermon and the whole thing sounds just like that. Would hearing that sermon make you feel like dancing as you walk out of church on Sunday morning?

Or what about some of the hymns we casually sing without really considering the words because they're so familiar to us? About the same time Jonathan Edwards was writing his famous sermon, Isaac Watts was writing this beloved hymn:

Alas! And did my Savior bleed,
And did my sovereign die?
Would He devote that sacred head
For such a worm as I? [4]

Worm! Are you a worm to God? Did Jesus die for worms or for people, God's highest creation whom he loves? People, that's whom Jesus died for, that's whom God loves! And he died not just for generalized, nameless people, but for you and me personally. In everything Jesus said and did, from his birth to his death on the cross, your name was precious to him and was hidden in his

3 Jonathan Edwards, sermon, "Sinners in the Hands of an Angry God," (Boston: S. Kneeland and T. Green, 1741).

4 Isaac Watts, hymn, "Alas! And Did My Savior Bleed?" in Inspiring Hymns (Grand Rapids: Singspiration Music, a Division of Zondervan Corporation, 1974) # 93. In the public domain.

heart. And it's still there. What reassurance! What comfort! I can dance with such knowledge. Can't you?

As a pastor, counselor and chaplain, I've often visited with people who were so overwhelmed with feelings of guilt and unworthiness they didn't feel much like dancing. If a bad thing happened to them, they thought God was punishing them for something they'd done. He wasn't, but that's how they felt. For them and all of us, the good news is that the war between God and sinners ended at the cross. In love, Jesus died there for the sins of the world. That means God is not mad at anyone. In fact, *he's in love with us*! All of life is simply our opportunity to discover God's love.

"Peace be with you!" the risen Jesus told the frightened, guilt-plagued disciples in the upper room on the first Easter Sunday. Three times Jesus told them that! He doesn't say, "You loathsome insects! You worms! Aren't you ashamed of yourselves for running out on me?" No, three times he said, "Peace be with you!" (John 19:20, 21, 26).

You are not a loathsome insect or worm, despite the songs you've sung or the sermons you might have heard! You are a beloved child of God for whom Jesus died. "For God so loved the world that he gave his only Son...." You and I are the world and God loves us! If you can joyfully shout "I'm a beloved child of God!" then you've had an epiphany about who you are. You've learned a joyful tune that can set your heart to dancing.

Now, yes, there were some people Jesus addressed some harsh words to. "You are of your father the devil, and your will is to do your father's desires," Jesus told the Pharisees (John 8:44a). In another place Jesus repeatedly addressed the scribes and Pharisees as "blind guides" and "hypocrites." "You snakes! You brood of vipers!" he said to them. "How will you escape being condemned to hell?" (Matthew 23). Hmmm — do I detect similarities to Jonathan Edwards? It almost sounds like it. But, no, that's not it at all.

Why then did Jesus speak this way to religious leaders, the good people of the day? He spoke to them that way because they were proud, arrogant and self-righteous. They thought they were sinless, perfect in every way, model citizens in the kingdom of God. And they looked down their noses at everyone else.

There's an old saying, "Pride is a disease that makes everyone sick but the person who has it." That's who the Pharisees were, people infected with arrogance and pride. They and the scribes are the only people Jesus ever spoke this harshly to. He never spoke this way to the prostitutes, the tax collectors, the lepers, the blind, the poor, the widows, the epileptics.

Why? Because they weren't phonies. They didn't present themselves as something they weren't. They were humble people who recognized their faults and sought the mercy and love of Jesus. I believe that includes you. If it didn't, if you thought you were already perfect, you wouldn't be taking the time to read this today.

I've met a few scribes, Pharisees, and hypocrites. But they were not among those weeping in my office, or looking frightened on their hospital beds, or the ones holding my hand as they lay dying. These hurting people rejoiced when reassured of God's love for them. Even if their eyes were full of tears, their hearts were often dancing when we parted.

So, let's clear the dance floor of all this worm and loathsome insect business and rejoice in the knowledge of how precious each of one of us is to God. But there's much more to dance about. There's the unique personality, the abilities, the talents, the physical features, the likes and dislikes, the special gifts each one of us has from God. These are the things that make us true individuals, different from anyone else on the planet.

When I was in junior high school and high school, I was probably the worst athlete in every physical education class. I couldn't run. I couldn't catch balls. I couldn't hit balls. I couldn't dribble. I couldn't make a basket if my life depended on it.

I remember the humiliation I experienced when they chose up sides for teams. "You take Neidigk," someone would say. "No! You take him; we had him last time." I was always the last one on the bench, along with Philip, an overweight boy who became a close friend. No one wanted him either. To spare myself the humiliation of rejection, I'd often volunteer to be the referee.

Nobody liked the referee, but at least as referee I wouldn't make a touchdown for the other side. I actually did that once.

So, sports weren't my thing. But writing was. In high school I enrolled in journalism and within a year, I was the editor of the school paper. I enrolled in literary magazine, and the next thing you know, I was the editor of that too. I took a broadcast news class in college, and by the end of my freshman year, I was the news director for the campus radio station. God hadn't blessed me with the coordination or lungs of an athlete, but he did bless me with a creative mind that could write and edit. That's who I was. That gave me joy.

I discovered I was passionate about helping the needy. During high school food drives I collected hundreds of pounds of canned goods and meat and donated it to the Salvation Army. I discovered I could listen and talk to people about their problems. I gathered a group of "project friends," I called them, people no one liked but who needed to be loved and have their stories heard. So, I'd often hang out with them and try to encourage them.

These kinds of abilities and interests helped me build a picture of my identity, and how God wanted me to be in the world. From high school on, I've pretty much always been that way. I've been a caring person. I've used my talents as a writer for my own enjoyment and the benefit of others. And guess what? That's exactly what ended up in my personal life plan that I put down on paper for the first time a decade and a half ago. Knowing who I am and how God has blessed me and then acting on that knowledge has helped me dance; it's become a source of joy. It's when I stray from that, that I'm not happy.

"What is man that you are mindful of him, and the Son of Man that you care for him?" the psalmist asks (Psalm 8:4). Or, to make it very personal, put your own name in the place of "man." "What is _____ that God is mindful of him (or her)?" Well, you and I just happen to be the highest and most beloved creatures of God. We didn't have to do anything to earn that status. That's who God made us to be. We're just a little lower than the angels, at least for the moment. Angels are in heaven and can see God. We're here, and though God is everywhere around us, we can't see him. At least, I've never seen him.

Even so, in many ways you and I are far superior to angels. The Bible says God sends angels to be our helpers (Hebrews 1:14). But nowhere does the Bible say God loves angels, though he says in many places he loves us. Nor does the Bible say anywhere that angels were made in God's image. But we are. And though the angels are holy and powerful, nowhere does the Bible say God's Son Jesus died to save them when they fell. But Jesus did die to save us, affirming our great value and worth to God. If you believe this, you can dance with who you are.

Often I meet people engaged in self-destructive behavior; drug and alcohol abuse, hurtful relationships, cutting, bulimia, anorexia — it's a long list. Why do people do this to themselves? Sometimes it's because they've been abused by someone else. Maybe they've had parents whom they never could please. Or sometimes they've listened to messages from the entertainment industry that tells them how they have to look or behave. They try, but they can't measure up to these impossible standards so they hate themselves. Or they have a boyfriend or girlfriend or a spouse who constantly berates them. When someone believes these false messages, it can crush the spirit and lead to self-loathing and self-harm.

Part of healing is rejecting these negative messages and replacing them with the healing message of God's love and the healthy self-love that springs from it. To everyone who loathes himself, God says, "I don't loathe you. I love you. You're my precious child. I created you to spend your life rejoicing with me. I've sent my son to lift you up, to free you from mire so you can dance with me forever."

As a child of God, know that there's a wonderful, beautiful person inside you, created to be like your heavenly Father, a person that wants to dance. Don't accept the chains that the scribes, Pharisees, and hypocrites would place on you, chains that drag you down and keep you off the dance floor. Don't listen to the negative voices. You don't have to be anyone's doormat or whipping boy. Be what you are, a proud eagle released from its cage when Jesus broke your chains in his resurrection power, setting you free to soar.

Remember this song by Charles Wesley? It's called "Amazing Love." It is still under copyright law, but look it up or listen to it online. It describes being freed.

That happened to an older woman in Kansas. I remember when her chains fell off. She had been married to a harsh and demanding old-school immigrant from Eastern Europe. I visited her from time to time. I'll call her Greta. Her husband's name was Pete. Whenever I visited, Pete did all the talking. Greta was as quiet and meek as a mouse. She wouldn't even look up. She seemed to have no personality or will whatsoever. She never left the house. Pete ran all the errands. Then Pete died.

Within days it was as though Greta had broken out of a dungeon. She was happy. She was out and about in the community. She chattered constantly. She started making bright clothing and decorations. She seemed a different person. But she wasn't really. She was the same person she'd always been but now that person inside her was unchained. What a beautiful butterfly she really was! I'm so sad that it took the death of Pete for Greta to find her voice and begin dancing with who she was. But she did find herself, and she discovered she was worth dancing about.

Are you dancing with who you are? What a joyful life can be yours as you embrace God's love for you in Christ and the person he created you to be! It's never too late to dance!

Dance Steps — Questions For Reflection

1. What is there about yourself that other people might be surprised to learn? This could be something you've done, an ability you have, a hobby you enjoy, or...?
2. If Jesus appeared to you right now, how might he greet you? Would he be scolding, welcoming, comforting, encouraging, or something else? Why?
3. Think of an animal, flower, bird, or insect that best describes the person you are, or would like to be. Why did you choose that particular creature?
4. Whom would you rather have lunch with: a prostitute, leper, epileptic, suicide survivor, Pharisee, or priest? Why might it be hard to have lunch with any of these? Or would it?
5. When you look in the mirror do you see someone you love, someone you dislike, someone you think is beautiful, or someone you think is ugly? How do you think God sees you?
6. How are you important to others? If you were gone for a year, what would they miss most about you? What would you most miss about them?
7. Should children have to earn the love of their parents? If not, do you sometimes think you have to earn the love of your heavenly Father? Why, or why not?
8. Why do you think some people intentionally hurt themselves? What could you say or do to help someone inclined to do this?
9. Do you sometimes think you have to let people abuse you physically, sexually, emotionally, verbally, or in any other way? Why? If you feel you are in danger, do you have a Plan B, that is a safe place to go, or a safe person you can talk to?
10. How will your thinking about yourself have to change if you are to feel freer to dance?
11. Think of someone you can encourage today to help them feel more like dancing. Who will that be? What will you tell them?

The Third Dance Step To Joy — Dance With Those You Love

"The poor you will have with you always. You will not always have me." Matthew 26:11

Do you remember the old Burma-Shave roadside jingles? Six billboards would be placed along the highway, each with a word or two from a rhyme. The last sign would say, "Burma-Shave." Here's one I remember. "If daisies are your favorite flower, keep pushing up those miles per hour. Burma-Shave." A commercial disguised as a public service announcement — how clever! But couldn't there be a happier way to sell shaving cream than the fear of death?

You'd think the fear of death would be more appropriate for an evangelistic message. At least that's a common motive for "getting religion." And sure enough, someone in Texas, inspired by the Burma-Shave signs, came up with this roadside jingle I saw years ago: "Life is short. Death is sure. Sin the cause. Christ the cure." That's using fear as a motive for conversion. It worked for Phil, a college friend of mine. Once I asked him, "Phil, why did you become a Christian?" His reply, "I didn't want to go to hell."

The fear of death seems to be behind much religious messaging. But fear is not joy. And fear doesn't lead to dancing. But love does! Sure, death is inevitable, but rather than just using the fear of it as the primary motive for getting religion, why not let the shortness of life be a powerful motive for loving the people who matter most to us? We may not be here tomorrow. Sharing and receiving love isn't something to be put off. Love is to be celebrated and nurtured and enjoyed to the fullest extent, now. Today is the day for dancing! No one knows what tomorrow will bring. Life is a limited time opportunity to dance with those you love.

Let me give you an example. Years ago, I met a retired pastor in Arizona. He and his first wife spent their entire married life doing church work. Now church work is good; don't misunderstand me. It needs to be done. And this couple felt duty bound to do it. But church work is what they did almost every day of their married life. Every day was devoted to organizing church events and spending time with church people. They always said to each other, "When we retire, we'll have some fun together." The joy of their dance was always in the future.

They retired. At last they could dance! But within a year, the pastor's wife was diagnosed with cancer and she died. Her husband was devastated. Not only did he grieve her death, he grieved the loss of the "fun" they were going to have but never got around to. Somehow, they always managed to put off going to the dance.

By the time I met him, this retired pastor had remarried. We were eating lunch at the same table during a break at a conference in Arizona. Clearly, he was in a hurry. He wasn't sticking around for the meetings. He and his new wife were heading out to do some sightseeing. He wasn't about to waste the time he had left sitting in on some boring lecture or attending a business meeting.

Bravo for him! He was going to do some serious dancing. By that I mean he was going to rejoice in his bride, this woman he loved, and they were going to have some fun together. Yes, he and his new wife were well along in years, but it wasn't too late for them to dance.

They remind me of another couple who attended a blind support group I facilitated. Bill and Betty were both widowed. They had known and liked each other for many years before they lost their spouses. And now they continued to be friends. At one of the meetings for blind people, Bill and Betty announced that they were now an "item." Bill followed it up by saying, "Dorothy and I had 69 wonderful years together. I don't expect Betty and I will get anywhere near that. Heck, I'd be happy with six months." That was a man who knew how to dance! Both in their nineties with not much time left, he and Betty planned to squeeze in all the joy they could. It's never too late to dance.

But for some reason, many of us are like that retired pastor before his first wife died. We put off the joy of the dance because we think the work we do is more important. Is it really? Can't our work sometimes wait? Won't people with needs always be there? Yes, they will, but the ones we cherish won't. The time to love them is limited. The time to dance is now. As Jesus said, "The poor you will have with you always. You will not always have me" (Matthew 26:11). The poor were important to Jesus. But the love he shared with his closest friends and disciples was more important.

Whatever our calling, we deal with people. Our clientele are important. Church members are important to church workers. Customers are important to business owners. Students are important to teachers. Patients are important to caregivers. Some of these people will have greater needs than others. And we will do our best to help them meet their needs. That's our calling. That's our job.

But they're going to step in and out of our lives, and different people with more needs will come along. But who really needs to take first place: our ever coming and going clientele, or the people we care about most? Isn't it the people we cherish who deserve the greatest and best portion of our time, emotion, energy and money? All relationships are temporary. But our loved ones are our real treasures. Dancing with our loved ones at every important moment in life is what really matters. It's taken me years to figure this out.

It's time for *True Confessions*. That's actually the name of a magazine from years ago which featured people sharing their embarrassing stories before the whole world. Maybe you paged through a copy while waiting to check out at the grocery store. I haven't seen one for a long time. Maybe the "Jerry Springer Show" has replaced it. With a red face, let me share with you just one example of misplaced priorities in my own life.

This story is so outrageous I could never make it up. My wife was in the hospital delivery room about to give birth to our son. A messenger came to the door of the delivery room to tell me a member of the church was waiting outside to see me. You guessed it. I left my wife there on the table in the delivery room and went out to the waiting area to speak to this church member. I barely made it back for the birth of our child. Why Kathy didn't shoot me, I'll never know.

All those people — most of them church people — who were once so important that I neglected my family's needs to meet theirs, are long gone. Many have died, moved, transferred to other churches or dropped out altogether. Maybe I had a positive impact on their lives. Maybe I didn't. Meanwhile, my family often didn't receive the love and attention from me they deserved. I wish I could go back and do some things over. I can't. I can only learn from my mistakes and use the time I have left to dance with the people I love.

Fortunately, my Christian faith is centered on the grace and forgiveness of God through Jesus Christ. I'm reminded of the story of a sinful woman who crashed a party Jesus attended that he'd been given by a Pharisee. The woman, uninvited, fell at the feet of Jesus, drenching them with her tears and drying them with her hair. The Pharisee was disgusted. But Jesus said, "Her sins, which are many, are forgiven — for she loved much. But he who is forgiven little, loves little." And he said to the woman, "Your faith has saved you; go in peace" (Luke 7:47-48, 50).

You and I are like this unnamed woman. As the years pass and we reflect on our lives, we realize how short we've fallen, not only of God's standards but our own. Perhaps we've become overwhelmed with remorse and guilt. We wish we could be like Superman and spin time and the world backward so we can do things over. That's not possible, but by faith we can receive the understanding, the acceptance, the mercy, the forgiveness of Jesus. And as we do, we experience his peace.

"Peace I leave with you; my peace I give to you; not as the world gives do I give to you. Do not let your heart be troubled, nor let it be fearful," says our Lord to his disciples (John 14:27). The Christian faith is not about berating oneself and wallowing in guilt. It's about basking in the warm glow of God's grace, forgiveness, and peace given to us freely through Jesus Christ.

The Third Dance Step

If you're like me, you're eager to grant the grace, forgiveness, and peace of God to others. But you have a hard time drinking deeply of it for yourself. You spend a lot of emotional energy beating yourself up for your shortcomings. But beating yourself up doesn't fix anything. It doesn't lead to joy. Living in God's grace, forgiveness, and peace does. Take all you need! You can never take too much. It's a bottomless well. There's always more. There's no danger of God suffering from compassion fatigue and running out of what you need. Drink deeply and then get back in the dance.

Viktor Frankl, a Holocaust survivor and famous psychiatrist, said in his book, *Man's Search for Meaning*, that every day in the concentration camps he asked himself, "Is this the first day of the rest of your life or the last day of your life so far?"[5]

This very moment, Frankl seems to suggest, is a fresh opportunity to live differently. With Frankl's encouragement and the words of Jesus fresh in our minds, now is the perfect time to dance into a new beginning.

I can't go back and attend all the track meets and football games I missed that my sons participated in as high school boys. But I can call or text them now. And I can attend the special events in their lives as adults that are happening today. I can be present for what's important to my grandchildren. I can start loving my wife today in whatever ways she perceives is loving and caring.

I think that's crucial. It's important to love those we really care about in ways they perceive as loving. My wife Kathy inherited her parents' old farmhouse in Mesilla Park, New Mexico. We spent some of our happiest moments as a married couple working on this house and making it homey and livable. And let me tell you, it was a real disaster when we got it. A contractor we hired asked me, "Did this used to be a barn?" No, it had never been a barn.

Not only the house, but the yard was a never-ending problem. It was huge and needed to be watered. Every summer during our vacations, Kathy would drag hundreds of feet of garden hose all around to water the grass and shrubs. Every half hour or so she would go out and drag a sprinkler to a different spot. It was hot, dirty work.

5 Viktor Frankl, *Man's Search for Meaning* (Boston: Beacon Press, 2006).

So, one day I bought Kathy a birthday present. I wrapped it up beautifully and gave it to her. When she opened it, she looked at it and said absolutely nothing. Now if I had gotten it for a birthday present, I would have been delighted. My heart would have danced. But Kathy didn't dance. She just sat there and said nothing. Clearly something was wrong. What could possibly be wrong? My gift was something she did not perceive of as loving; that's what was wrong.

It was a lawn sprinkler tractor painted in John Deere colors, yellow and green. I thought it was just what she needed. You screw it on to the hose, turn on the water, and as the sprinkler head goes round and round, the tractor crawls across the yard. You can set it up and a few hours later the yard is watered and you just shut off the hose. No work required. But Kathy was not pleased. She said nothing.

You see, it was something she could use but not something she wanted. Eventually she spoke up. She told me she would much rather have some new gold earrings and a nice dinner at Red Lobster. That was the sort of present that she would perceive of as loving and would set her heart to dancing. So, I took the John Deere tractor-sprinkler back to the hardware store and gave her the earrings she wanted.

How do your loved ones want to be loved? You probably already know. After living with someone for years, you have a good idea of what gives them joy. But guys aren't always as sensitive about such things as we should be. Some women aren't either. And adults don't necessarily know how kids want to be loved. So, if you don't know, ask! Just say something like, "How can I show my love for you in ways that would make you feel loved?"

The answer is probably not going to be something complicated and expensive. You don't necessarily have to spend thousands of dollars on a cruise. You don't have come up with something that takes hours and weeks of planning. The more complicated and expensive, the less likely it is you'll do it. Sometimes love is just being present; it's just being there. It's taking a walk together. It's going to the park with your grandkids. It's sitting on the couch watching a movie, eating microwave popcorn. It's painting a bedroom together. It's finding a big cardboard box and letting the grandkids play in it. It's doing a jigsaw puzzle together for a few minutes every day till it's done. The key is: Keep it simple. Keep it spontaneous. And whatever it is, do it often.

A few decades ago, "quality time" was all the rage. We were all so busy we didn't have time for our loved ones, so we were told that what little time we had with them should be "quality time." And quality time involved scheduling and planning.[6]

So, maybe once a week would be family night. We wouldn't schedule meetings. We wouldn't attend school related activities. There'd be no staying late at the office or bringing work home. We wouldn't even go to church that night. Quality time took first place for that one or two hours every week. It's not a totally bad idea. We need happy things to look forward to. But quality time is really no replacement for just plain and simple time.

It's when we're just sharing extended moments with the people we love that real intimacy happens. Important conversations don't necessarily happen all at once. Sometimes the little details, the meaningful observations, the important reflections that bring us together, the needs of our heart we want to share but haven't been able to speak, trickle out slowly. It can take an entire day or two or three for that to happen. It can't be scheduled. It requires being present and available.

Suppose you and a loved one have a problem communicating. Maybe your spouse feels ignored. So, as you breeze by each other, she or he says, "You never listen to me. We don't ever talk." You pause for a moment and reply, "Okay, I'm listening. Talk."

What's going to happen? Probably nothing. "Well, I can't think of anything to say right now," your spouse replies. So, you just hurry off and say, "Well, let me know when you come up with something." Time — not planned and scheduled quality time, but just time — is what nurtures and encourages real exchanges from the heart. Then, when it happens, you feel loved, you rejoice, and your heart dances.

6 Gary Chapman, *Five Love Languages: How to Express Heartfelt Commitment to Your Mate* (Chicago: Northfield Publishing, 1995).

To have that kind of time with the people you love, you sometimes have to put some distance between you and the people you love less. Some might find that statement troubling. It's hard to say "No" to people who need your help and whom you care about in order to say "Yes" to people you love more. It can feel unkind, almost mean.

But that's what Jesus did. It may be hard for us to hear this, but Jesus didn't love everybody equally. Jesus loved the crowds of people who followed him, and he would sometimes deprive himself of food and rest to care for them. But sometimes he would just leave. He would go off by himself and take only his twelve disciples with him so he could spend time with just them. But even among his disciples, there were three whom Jesus loved more than the others. You probably know their names; Peter, James, and John.

And among those three, there was just one who is called "the disciple Jesus loved," John. Six times John is called "the disciple Jesus loved" (John 13:23; 19:26; 20:2; 20:8; 21:7; 21:20). It was John who leaned upon the breast of Jesus. It was John who stayed with Jesus from his arrest in the Garden of Gethsemane, through his many trials, through his crucifixion, and until the moment of his death. It was John to whom Jesus, as he hung dying on the cross, entrusted the care of his mother.

Do you remember the Smothers Brothers comedy and folk music duo? In one of their routines Tommy resentfully said to Dick, "Mom always liked you best." Maybe we feel guilty about it when we like someone best. But it's true; there are people we do like best. Maybe your mother liked your brother or sister best. There's probably a parent, sibling, friend, child, or uncle you like best too. Jesus liked John best. It's normal. And it's okay to dance with those we like best even if it means someone else has to wait their turn.

Moreover, whomever it is we choose to love, allowing them to love us back in ways they think it is loving is important for their joy too. So, we let them. Before Jesus went to Jerusalem to be crucified, he shared a meal with three of his closest friends — Martha, Mary, and Lazarus. During the meal, Mary poured an entire bottle of very expensive perfume all over Jesus' feet. The aroma filled the room. This was the sort of treasure a woman would save for her wedding day, but Mary chose this occasion to anoint Jesus's feet with it.

Judas Iscariot was angered by this. "Why wasn't this perfume sold and the money given to the poor?" he demanded.

Jesus put him in his place. "Leave her alone. This was done in preparation for the day of my burial." Then he went on to say, "The poor you have with you always. You will not always have me" (John 12:1-7).

It made Mary's heart dance with joy to share with someone she deeply loved her most treasured possession. It was even more important for her to do this because she realized something no one else in the room would admit, that time with Jesus was limited. So, she used what limited time she had to give of her best to the one she really loved. She would never regret what she did. Despite how impractical her gift was, she would always have the memory of that last dance with Jesus.

I believe God would have us share our most treasured possession, our limited time in this world, with those we love. Today is a wonderful day for dancing with them. As long as we have each other, it's never too late to dance.

Dance Steps — Questions For Reflection

1. Is fear or love of God a greater motivator for you in matters of faith? Why?
2. If you could turn back the clock, how would your relationship with loved ones who have died be different?
3. Who are your closest loved ones? Ask one of them this week, "How can I best show my love for you?" What might they say?
4. When have you placed business, co-workers, or clients before loved ones? How has this made you, and your loved ones, feel?
5. Why is it sometimes hard to say "No" to someone you don't really care that much about?
6. Many people have a hard time forgiving themselves. Do you? Why or why not?
7. Do you look at your life as a story of lost opportunities or new beginnings? Why?
8. If someone you love asks you how you want to be loved today, what will you say?
9. Which do you enjoy most, planned or spontaneous events with loved ones? What is your happiest memory of either one?
10. Does it bother you to realize someone you love might love someone else more than you? Why?
11. Whom do you especially love that you will do something special with this week? What will that be?

The Fourth Dance Step To Joy — Dance Free From That Rope!

"Someone in the crowd said to him, 'Teacher, tell my brother to divide the inheritance with me.' But he said to him, 'Man, who made me a judge or arbitrator over you?'" Luke 12:13-14

"Mission Impossible" — that's one of my favorite high drama TV shows from the late '60s and early '70s. You can catch old episodes with Peter Graves on YouTube, or you can rent the more recent versions with Tom Cruise.

Each episode began in a similar way. The hero, Jim, listened to a tape recording describing a corrupt politician or military megalomaniac who was out to create havoc and oppression in some far corner of the world. After laying out the background, the voice on the recording said, "Your mission, Jim, should you decide to accept it, is to stop General So-and-So." Then came the disclaimer, "As always, should you or any members of your I.M. force be caught or killed, the secretary will disavow any knowledge of your actions. This tape will self-destruct in five seconds. Good luck, Jim."[7]

Will Jim and his team take on the mission? Will they grab the rope and save the world? Well, obviously they did, week after week, or there wouldn't have been the long-running TV series. And they always completed their mission successfully. The secretary never had to disavow anything. Over and over, Peter Graves, Leonard Nimoy and the other members of the I.M. team solve impossible problems and rescue helpless innocent people in impossible situations. But they always have a choice to grab the rope or not. And so do we.

You and I have received phone calls, text messages, emails — and maybe even a few in-person requests — from people who want to give us a mission we don't have on our calendars

7 Bruce Geller, American television spy series, "Mission Impossible", starring Peter Graves, (Culver CA: Desi-Lu Studios, 1966-1973).

and probably don't really want. Usually, they're small requests. We're not being asked to stop a brutal dictator in his tracks. It's more like "Will you take care of my dogs for a week while I'm on vacation? And while you're at it, will you bring in the paper, pick up the mail, and water my grass?"

If it's a member of my family or a close friend and it's a reciprocal kind of thing sometimes I'll say "Yes". If I can give someone I care about space to go dancing — so they can get away for a joyful time of rest and relaxation, I'll grab the rope. I may be inconvenienced for a few days, but I'm pretty confident that in the future, the favor will be returned allowing me to go dancing too.

But beyond those little jobs, the rope can get heavier and longer and involve people I'm not really close to if I let it. I've been asked to take an elderly person to a doctor's office, or bring groceries to a person with no car, or help someone move furniture. I don't mind doing that occasionally, but if it becomes a pattern, if I figure out that someone has designated me to be their free taxi driver, delivery person, or mover, I'm inclined to say "No." I'm especially inclined to say "No" if the person requesting help has the means of helping themselves but just doesn't want to spend the money. I remember a sticker I saw once in the back window of a pickup truck. It said, "Yes, this is my truck. No, I won't help you move."

From rude impositions to serious requests for major assistance, the ropes people throw us can become life changing commitments if we grab them. As a pastor, I'm generally considered a trustworthy person. For that reason, several church members over the years have asked me to hold their financial or medical power-of-attorney or to be the executor of their estates. That's certainly a vote of confidence, but that's not my role. And it's a potentially huge and time-consuming responsibility. So, I've politely danced away from their rope. When I can, I've made some suggestions as to who might take on these important jobs for them.

Saying "No" when someone throws you a rope can seem like a mean and unloving thing to do. How can you refuse someone's cry for help when you have it in your power to assist them? To say "No" can leave one feeling profoundly guilty. If you've read the Christian classic, *In His Steps* by Charles Sheldon, you might feel even guiltier saying "No." Sheldon's premise is that we should always ask ourselves, "What would Jesus do?" The implied answer is that Jesus would say "Yes" to requests for help, so we should do the same.[8]

But if we have that understanding, we'll find ourselves hung by a rope of our own choosing till dead. We may be dancing, but it will be at the end of someone else's rope.

Jesus had no problem saying "No" when it conflicted with his understanding of who he was and what he'd come to do. So, who was he, and what did he come to do? According to Jesus, "the Son of Man came to seek and to save the lost" (Luke 19:10). In another place, Jesus said, "the Son of Man came not to be served but to serve, and to give his life as a ransom for many" (Mark 10:45). And, "I have come down from heaven, not to do my own will but the will of him who sent me" (John 6:38).

That was the Son of God's personal life plan; doing his Father's will, serving and saving the lost, and giving his life as a ransom. If a need presented itself that didn't fit his life plan, Jesus felt no sense of obligation to meet it. And he didn't feel guilty when he said "No."

There's a great example of Jesus saying "No" when a request didn't fit his life plan. He's in the midst of a large crowd preaching an extended sermon about a variety of profound topics. Halfway through, someone yells out, "Teacher, tell my brother to divide the inheritance with me." Jesus replies, "Man, who made me a judge or arbitrator over you?" (Luke 12:13-14). Or, put another way, Jesus is saying, "Sorry, but I'm not the probate judge. I'm not grabbing that rope."

Apparently, a real injustice was taking place. A greedy brother was depriving this sibling of his share of the property. How unfair! Someone ought to step in help this victim of injustice! But being an arbitrator in an inheritance dispute wasn't Jesus's calling. If the man had a legitimate complaint against his brother,

8 Charles Sheldon, *In His Steps* (Chicago: Chicago Advance, 1896).

he could hire a lawyer. Jesus wasn't available for that kind of work. Jesus came to seek and to save the lost and give his life as a ransom for many. So, Jesus said "No."

It's okay for us to dance away from the rope, even as Jesus did. If you can't say "No," if you try to meet every request for help that comes your way, you'll exhaust yourself physically and emotionally and possibly die in poverty. I've known several tenderhearted people who did just that, forcing themselves onto public assistance. And that doesn't lead to anyone dancing.

Joy comes from knowing who you are, why you're here, and sticking to your life plan. So how can you know if a rope thrown your way is one you should grab, or one you should happily dance away from with no feelings of guilt at all? Here are two questions you can ask yourself that can serve as a filter:

First, ask yourself, "Is this a rope I'm morally obligated to grab?" Or put another way, "Is there direction from the Bible, my church, and my deeply held values that apply to this situation? Does my spiritually formed conscience say this is something I must do?" If not, you can simply dance away from the rope. But if your moral compass and life plan guide you to say, "Yes, I must do this," then grab the rope with joyful enthusiasm and dance with it wherever it leads.

That's how the good Samaritan saw his responsibility. You probably remember this beloved parable of Jesus. A Samaritan, confronted with a wounded and dying man on a remote stretch of road, treated the man's wounds, packed him out on his donkey, and put him up in an inn at his own expense. Earlier, a priest and a Levite, respected religious leaders, had walked around the man, ignoring his need, but not the Samaritan. He followed his moral compass and acted as a loving neighbor to a man who would die without his help. After telling the story, Jesus said, "You go and do likewise" (Luke 10:25-37).

When someone is a helpless victim and will likely die or suffer severe harm without my assistance, I'm morally obligated to be his neighbor and help however I can, unless it jeopardizes my duty to protect and care for my own family. But I'm not morally obligated to help someone with problems that is not in grave danger.

A homeless person may touch my heartstrings with his sign that reads, "Homeless vet. Please help." But that doesn't mean I have to give him a handout. Perhaps I can be more helpful by donating money to a local shelter for homeless vets and letting him know where to find it.

A woman has a Facebook friend she's never really met who needs a kidney transplant. "My friend will die if I don't donate my kidney," she told me. She thinks she's a compatible donor. But donating a kidney is risky. Her life could be shortened. She might even die. But she's sure her friend will die soon if she doesn't donate her kidney. What should she do?

I pointed out to her that unless she has a direct line to God, she has no idea when and why her friend might die. Then I reminded her that she's the sole caregiver for her disabled, elderly father. Who will take care of him if the surgery goes badly? Moreover, her daughter and son-in-law are struggling financially and live with her. If she's not around, they could become homeless.

So, should she donate the kidney or not? Frankly, there's no easy answer. It's okay to donate the kidney if she wanted to. It's also okay not to donate. But in my view, caring for her immediate family may be the greater, more immediate moral obligation. If she decided not to donate, if she chose to dance away from the rope, there is no guilt imposed on her. Staying alive to care for her own family would mean her whole household could keep dancing.

The second question you can ask yourself is, "Will I feel resentful if I grab this rope?" I'm an expert on resentment having grabbed countless ropes I didn't have to grab. Usually, my goal was to help someone, usually church members, avoid the embarrassment of failure and thus appear successful. But in so doing, I deprived them of opportunities to learn. Meanwhile, I'd be stuck typing up someone's business meeting minutes because they didn't have a computer or didn't know how to type or couldn't remember what happened in the meeting, and so on. But I wasn't the person who needed the learning experience. The individual whose rope I grabbed was.

As a pastor I've always wanted people to be successful and feel good about themselves. When unpleasant conversations needed to be had, I've tended to avoid them and simply tried to "be nice." Thus, if a paid or volunteer church worker was assigned a job but didn't do it, or perhaps did it poorly, I would step in and fix it or do it for them. Sometimes I did this without being asked. Sometimes I did it at their request. That way, public events would happen without incident, boards would have proper information and documents for meetings, the church would be clean and in good repair, refreshments would be served when needed, etc., and everyone would be spared the embarrassment and blame of not having done their work.

Over and over, I grabbed hold of the rope and became the rescuer. The people charged with the job would come off smelling like roses, and I would be left fuming in a stew of resentment. I did this for years. I didn't need to. I could have just said, "No." After all, it wasn't my responsibility. Sometimes I would try to dance away from the rope, reminding people that my role was doing word and sacrament ministry and the role of the laity was doing everything else. But over and over I would wimp out and do someone else's work for them, putting myself and the congregation on a path to "mutually assured destruction," to use a phrase from the Cold War, otherwise known as MAD.

You can tell you're on the MAD path when you find yourself holding a rope that isn't yours and feeling increasingly angry and resentful as you do it. I've found Rabbi Edwin Friedman's book *The Failure of Nerve: Leadership in the Age of the Quick Fix*, insightful.[9]

It's the sort of book you should read at the beginning of your career, not decades into it. Friedman says it's not our job to relieve other people of anxiety and make them happy. Thinking that way is a recipe for creating our own inner pain and ultimate failure. Other people need to feel their own anxiety and unhappiness in order to learn and grow. It's not our job to deprive them of it.

If I think someone is not holding up his end of the stick, or has made a wrong decision that negatively impacts those he

9 Edwin Friedman, *The Failure of Nerve: Leadership in the Age of the Quick Fix* (New York: Church Publishing, 2017).

works with, my job is to tell him so, not do his work for him. I don't need to cover up for him or agree with him to make him happy. All that does is breed anger and resentment in me. When I'm resentful, the joy is sucked out of me and I don't feel like dancing. But when I speak the truth in love and dance away from the rope that rightfully belongs to someone else, I can live with my conscience, have fewer stomach aches, sleep better at night and be ready to dance tomorrow.

Dancing away from the rope takes nerve. It takes backbone. And where do we get that? It comes from realizing that there's a difference between real guilt and false guilt. Real guilt is incurred when we do something, or fail to do something, in violation of our conscience. By conscience, I mean the moral anchor that has been deeply formed in us by our encounters with God through his word, either his written word or his word imprinted on our hearts.

False guilt is feeling badly that we do or say something that hurts someone's feelings, or makes them uncomfortable, or gives them a moment of unhappiness, or angers them when we are in fact simply being truthful. That sort of guilt has nothing to do with truth. It's false guilt. Ignore it. If someone's feelings are hurt when all you have done is be truthful, it's their problem, not yours. You don't need to violate your own moral compass and grab their rope to keep them from crying.

In my hospital chaplaincy training, the residents read together Rabbi Friedman's "Fable of the Bridge."[10] You can find it in several places on the internet. Here's the gist of it:

A man struggles to find purpose and direction in his life. At last he realizes what he wants and needs. So, he sets off on a journey toward his goal. On the way he must cross a bridge. In the middle of the bridge is a stranger with a rope tied around his waist. Without warning or explanation, the stranger throws the traveler the end of the rope and jumps off the bridge.

"Just hold on," he yells as he goes over the side.

Instinctively, the traveler grabs the rope. The rope is too short to reach the bottom and the weight of the falling man drags the

---

10 Edwin Friedman, *Friedman's Fables* (New York: The Guilford Press, 1990).

traveler to the edge of the bridge.

"If you let go, I'll be lost," cries the stranger.

This is not what the traveler had in mind at all. The other man refuses to climb the rope to safety and the traveler isn't strong enough to pull him up. He waits hours for someone to come by and help. No one does. He's getting tired.

Meanwhile, the stranger yells, "My life is in your hands."

Eventually the traveler tells the other man, "I will not accept the position of choice for your life, only for my own; the position of choice for your own life, I hereby give back to you."

"What do you mean?" the other man asks, afraid.

"I mean, simply, it's up to you. You decide which way this ends. I will help you if you help yourself."

"You cannot mean what you say," the other man shrieks. "You would not be so selfish. I am your responsibility. What could be so important that you would let someone die? Do not do this to me."

The traveler states again, "I will not stand here and hold this rope. If you want to live, you must start moving now, and I will help you. Please, start now."

He waited a few minutes, but there was no change in the tension of the rope. "I accept your choice," the man said, at last, and freed his hands.[11]

Today, you and I are free people. We have been delivered from every rope of sin and death, fear and guilt by faith. Guided by God's word we are free to make whatever choices will result in genuine good for ourselves and our neighbor. How will we use this marvelous freedom? Will we use it to carry burdens even Jesus would reject? Or will we use our glorious freedom to dance? I'd rather use it to dance. And it's never too late to dance.

11 Edwin Friedman, *Friedman's Fables* (New York: The Guilford Press, 1990).

Dance Steps — Questions For Reflection

1. What ropes have you grabbed that made you feel resentful? Why didn't you say *No*?
2. How much influence will you let Charles Sheldon's question, "What would Jesus do?" have on your decision to grab someone's rope, or dance away from it? Why?
3. If someone asks you for help to resolve an inheritance dispute or take sides in a divorce case, what will you do? What will guide your decision to grab their rope or dance away from it?
4. Why does saying "No" to requests for help sometimes leave us feeling guilty?
5. How can you tell the difference between real guilt and false guilt in your life?
6. What ropes have you grabbed and joyfully danced with? Why?
7. How is the story of the good Samaritan helping the injured man different from your turning down a request for help from a homeless person? Or is it?
8. Weekly, if not daily, you probably get appeals for financial help from charities. How do you decide which ones to help?
9. Under what circumstances would you donate a kidney or other tissue? When would you not? Why?
10. Who in your life right now is throwing you a rope? What will you do? Why?
11. Suppose you decide to dance away from a rope thrown to you by someone who habitually makes bad decisions, someone you've helped many times before. This time, he or she dies. Will you feel guilty or will you still be able to dance with a good conscience? Why?

The Fifth Dance Step To Joy — Dance As You Discover God

"O the depth of the riches of the wisdom and knowledge of God! How unsearchable are his judgments, and his ways beyond finding out! For who has known the mind of the Lord?" Romans 11:33-34a

It was a hot Saturday in June. I was sitting cross-legged on my patio fixing my gas grill. That's when Elly, my four-year-old granddaughter, bounced over to me holding out a rock she had found.

"Look at this, Grandpa," she said, handing me the rock.

It was a milky white piece of quartz with a distinctly different brown finger of some other mineral embedded in it, almost like King Arthur's sword. "This was made a long time ago inside the earth, by a combination of heat and pressure. A volcano probably blew up and brought it to the surface of the earth," I explained as I turned the rock over and over and then gave it back to her.

"How do you know that?" Elly asked.

I paused for a moment, taken aback by this profound question from such a little girl.

"Actually, I don't," I admitted. "It's just the sort of thing they told me in school. But I really have no idea how this rock was made and where it came from."

With that, Elly dropped the rock and wandered off. When she handed me the rock, she had been dancing with joy in her discovery. But then, figuratively speaking, I popped her balloon with a cold explanation she hadn't asked for. I knew instantly I had blown an opportunity.

So a bit later I asked her about the rock, "Remember that rock you found?"

"Yes," she said.

"Why did you show it to me?"

Elly explained, "Because it was pretty. And I just wanted to. And I love you."

That was the spiritual moment I had missed earlier. Elly had been dancing with excitement when she brought me the rock, her heart was filled wonder, joy, and love. But with my unsought explanation I turned her joy into a soda without fizz. I should have kept my cold theories to myself and just asked her where she thought the rock came from, why it looked the way it did, and what she thought God might have to do with it. But instead of allowing her a joyful epiphany, I turned out the lights.

Portals of discovery of God and higher things are opening up for us all the time. They happen in all sorts of ways; in beautiful things we see, people we meet, conversations we have, as well as during quiet moments of contemplation. At any moment, we could be on the verge of a personal epiphany; an encounter with the divine and a new awareness of a sublime presence and power.

When we have these personal epiphanies, these "Wow!" moments of spiritual discovery, they can change us profoundly. They can transform our character, our behavior, our way of looking at the world, our understanding of the holy.

Perhaps you've had those moments. If you have, I suspect you wish you could have more of them. But sometimes the older and more educated and more sophisticated we get, the less frequently we have these experiences. Our appetite for wonder and discovery fades and we spend most of our time intellectualizing or just parroting what we heard someone else say.

How does that happen? I think it begins in childhood when we're taught the answers to profound questions we never had, rather than being encouraged to recognize our own questions. It's in countless random teachable moments that our awareness of God starts flickering to life and our first dance steps begin in our joyous discovery of the holy. When pastors and teachers pump sophisticated theology into kids' heads before there's even a question in their minds about such things, we dampen their natural spirit of curiosity, just as it is awakening to God. We quench the Spirit at the moment the flame of childlike faith beings to glow.

The first time I remember dancing in my discovery of God was during a church youth campout in Cloudcroft, New Mexico. We were roasting marshmallows around the camp fire. I was acting crazy, waving my flaming marshmallow around in the darkness when I smacked a girl named Sandy right in the face with it. She screamed and for a few panicked minutes I thought I had blinded her. But the pastor's wife, Mrs. London, "Fritz," her friends called her, cleaned Sandy's face with a cool wet cloth, she stopped crying and everything was okay again.

Everything, that is, except for me. I was shaking, and feeling tremendously guilty. That's when Mrs. London took me aside and explained to me that I wasn't guilty. Jesus had died for all my sins. That's what the cross was all about, she told me. At the cross God forgave me and he still loved me even now. I was overcome with relief and joy. For me, that was my first moment of encountering God in his grace and dancing with joy in my discovery. I'm sure I had heard it all before, but now for the first time it became personal and real for me.

A few years later, at New Mexico State University, from habit I suppose, I visited a church across the street to attend the worship service and then stayed for a Bible class for college students. The class members knew a lot more than I did and were dealing with serious theological issues. I remember throwing in my two cents worth about something in the discussion. Clearly, I said the wrong thing. Immediately, two members of the group pounced on me like a couple of vultures, correcting my erroneous point of view. I didn't say a thing after that.

Fortunately, I stuck with it, came back again and again, and found a couple of friends — Phil and Jon — who were also newbies when it came to their discovery and experience of God. We decided to read the Bible together and see what it had to say to us. Every Sunday afternoon we'd hike up to Las Cuevas, a big rock formation on the western slope of the Organ Mountains near Las Cruces. There we took turns reading aloud the entire book of Revelation. The designated reader would stand high atop the rock and read loudly to the two of us below. It was really quite dramatic.

Between readings we would sit together and talk about it. We could say anything we wanted to without fear of being scolded for having the wrong interpretation. I came away from those Sunday afternoons with my head and heart filled with visions and experiences of God I would never have otherwise had. There on the mountainside, my own little Mount Sinai, God revealed himself to me. I hiked up to the big rock, hot and tired when I got there. I came back down dancing, filled with joy, eager to share with someone else the God I had discovered.

On a mountainside, through the written word and conversation and prayer with my friends, I met God in his life changing power. It didn't hurt that I was also in the middle of creation's grandeur, with mountains shaped like organ pipes soaring above me, and the whole Rio Grande valley spread out beneath me. In seminary I would learn that what I was experiencing was the intersection of natural revelation and special revelation, one supporting and informing the other. But all I knew then was that I was discovering God and was rejoicing in the experience.

If I had only attended that Bible class for college students and nothing more, I suspect my interest and joy in discovering God would have evaporated. I may have come away with my head full of correct doctrine, but my heart might have remained empty of any personal discovery. Maybe I would have become nothing more than a Pharisee with answers for everything, including questions nobody asks. Or maybe I would have turned away from God altogether.

I think of the dozens of youth confirmation classes I've taught. Young people come to class brimming with excitement. They're full of questions they as yet don't know they're not supposed to ask. They boldly enter forbidden territory, wondering: "If God is so good, why does he let bad things happen?" "Are babies who aren't baptized saved?" "Do people who never heard of Jesus go to hell when they die?" "Why is it okay for my parents to do bad things but not me?" "Why is God so mean in the Old Testament but not in the New Testament?" "Why does church have to be so boring?" "How come people get blamed for things when God already planned it?"

You get the idea. The temptation is to deflect the question. More than once I've said something like, "We don't have time for that. Today we're covering the third petition of the Lord's Prayer. Bring it up later." But by the time "later" comes, the itch has gone and the opportunity to scratch and probe and discover God at the point of interest has vanished. I used to keep a list of such questions, thinking I could write a book with all the answers. But then, if anyone read it, it would drain out of them the wonder and curiosity and mystery and joy of discovering God for themselves. When you think you know all the answers, the dancing is over.

I've observed that for many, when the joy of personally discovering God is gone, so also is interest in church. I've baptized dozens of babies. Of these, I've seen fewer than half of them complete confirmation. Of those who are confirmed, a tiny fraction of them are still in church by the time they graduate from high school. The rest have lost all interest and concluded church has no relevance for them. I console myself in the hope that they'll check back in when they get married or have their own children. Maybe once upon a time they did this; not so much anymore in this post-Christian era.

People stay in their relationship with the church when there is an ongoing fresh and joyful discovery of God. My shut-in mother, Rhoda, still had a questioning mind and yearned for joyful experiences of God when she was 98 years old. Oh, she read the service orders and the sermons and devotional guides a friend brought her from church. But she often came away from them feeling like a deflated balloon or a pretzel with no salt. Maybe she should become a Catholic, she wondered aloud. She loved the mystery and pageantry of their liturgy. Maybe the Virgin Mary deserved more honor than her church gave her. Maybe there was more to sainthood than just being a Christian.

Something was missing for her. What was it? The missing ingredient was a joyful encounter with God in the company of friends who accepted the questioning mind she still had without trying to set her straight. Since there was no one who filled that role — my father once did — she felt she was not growing anymore but just withering away. Oh, how she would have loved to put on her dancing shoes again and have a freewheeling theological discussion that went wherever the conversation led!

So how do people like my mother, and the rest of us, get our dancing shoes back on? How do we go about joyfully discovering and experiencing God? To begin with, we need to know we have permission to experience God in all the ways he reveals himself; through the familiar words of the Bible, creeds, liturgy, and hymns, as well as through nature, the sacred moments in life, people we meet and the difficult questions and struggles of faith we encounter.

Recently, two friends and former members of my church, Bob and Jane, died. Before retirement, they lived for decades in a remote mountainous region of Arizona where Bob worked for the post office. Jane said that in Arizona they couldn't attend church because of the great distance they lived from town. But that was okay because they *"lived* in God's church."

Bob and Jane were both Christian people. As soon as they retired and moved to Rio Rancho, New Mexico, they became active church members. They believed in the Bible and the creeds and the sacraments. But as they would tell you, never were they apart from God because they lived in his temple, where he made known to them every day his power and beauty and love through his creation, a revelation of his presence that set their hearts dancing for decades.

I used to minimize and dismiss this kind of revelation. I don't anymore. The beauty of the creation is most certainly one of the ways God reveals himself. Saint Paul said, "For since the creation of the world [God's] invisible attributes, his eternal power and divine nature, have been clearly seen, being understood through what has been made..." (Romans 1:20 NAS).

No, the creation doesn't tell us about Jesus and his cross, but it most definitely points us to something beyond ourselves. Bob and Jane danced with joy in the God they encountered through his creation. But they also danced with God's people in their congregation when that became possible for them.

I've observed, and personally experienced through my own sorrow, that we can also discover God when we are most helpless, most alone, most fearful, and when we're in intense pain or dying. As a hospital chaplain I visited with many people in their suffering. Often, they wanted to talk about what they were feeling. They wanted to talk about where God was in all this. They wanted to see purpose and meaning in what was happening to them.

But friends and family often wouldn't allow it. "Don't tell him he's dying. It might frighten him. He might give up hope," they'd tell me. But what they were really saying was, "I'm uncomfortable with those things. I don't want to talk with him about it." So, when their loved one expressed his fears they'd say, "You're not dying; you'll be fine!" Thus, they'd paper over the distress of his heart and deprive him and themselves of sacred moments in the presence of God.

Some of my most exhilarating experiences have been at the bedside of someone terrified of death. It might have taken two or three visits before a patient felt confident enough to open up to me. But because I was willing to sit and listen and provide a safe space to talk, the sacred moments that came were abundant. I was privileged to journey with patients as they wrestled with questions they were afraid to ask. I heard sins confessed that had been buried for a lifetime. I was party to secrets shared that no one else but the patient, God, and I knew.

All these I call sacred moments. Time and again, within an hour or two of such visits, sometimes within minutes, the person I visited would die, slipping off into the next world, peacefully, perhaps with a bare hint of a smile. I would call that dancing.

Let no one discourage you from discovering God personally! Even if that happens in ways that don't always fit SOP — Standard Operating Procedure. Personally, I believe God's revelation of himself is objectively contained in holy scripture; that's my heritage from the reformation. It's also a way of looking at faith that's very consistent with hundreds of years of western European culture.

But feelings and emotions and experiences are important in our discovery of God too. In non-Western European cultures, such as the cultures of the native people of Latin America or Africa, miracles, wonders and signs have long been seen as powerful evidence of a supernatural presence.

In the book of Acts, miraculous events provide supporting evidence for the truth of the apostolic preaching. Through spoken word and witnessed wonders people were brought to faith, as they sensed the immediate presence of God. Why not today as well? Isn't God free to reveal himself in whatever ways he pleases? It also seems to me that God still reveals himself in ways that fit the culture and times of those seeking him.

One of my chaplaincy patients, a devout Catholic, was convinced that she had a personal angel named John. After her husband divorced her, leaving her with three small boys to raise alone, John appeared. He was present whenever she needed help, giving encouragement and guidance. Then when the boys were grown and gone, she saw less of John. But in the hospital, John reappeared, again encouraging her.

"He's right over there," she said, pointing toward the empty chair in the corner of the room. "You have an angel too. I can see him beside you. What's his name?"

I think I just sputtered like Porky Pig when she asked me this. "I guess I don't know," I answered, feeling very uncomfortable.

"Well, when you go home ask God to tell you his name, and then come back and tell me."

I didn't go home and ask God my angel's name. I wasn't convinced I had an angel. And I really didn't want one if I did have one. Having a personal angel was something foreign to my way of thinking. Theologically, I acknowledge the existence of angels, but they are not personally real to me. This woman made me realize there are some things to which I am just not open.

My experience of God and the spiritual world is much more conventional. I came to my faith after much searching and questioning, after conversing and arguing with people who held all sorts of beliefs, and unbeliefs. My discovery of God has been a very western European, and probably American experience. God met me in ways I'm comfortable with. And that's where I remain, although I confess I sometimes find my status quo boring. Sometimes when I realize I'm not dancing in my experience of God, I'm tempted to ask him my angel's name.

Maybe your experience is different from mine. I'm okay with that. I don't want you trying to duplicate my path to the kingdom of God. I want to leave you alone with God to work out your own unique experience of him. That's why I'm not going to tell you that you have to believe in God exactly the same way I do. I could tell you what I believe — I've actually done quite a bit of that already — but you'd still have to discover God for yourself. You don't have to live with what I believe. You have to live with what you believe.

Years ago, home from college on winter break in Hobbs, New Mexico, I attended the Christmas Eve service at the church I grew up in. After the service on the way out the door, I greeted Pastor London. I wanted him to tell me straight-up whether some of the things I had been taught were true. So, I asked him, "Pastor London, was Jesus really born of a virgin?"

"What do you think?" he replied.

But I didn't want to think! That's why I asked him the question. I wanted him to sign, seal and deliver my faith to me in a neat package. But he wouldn't do it. He forced me to wrestle with what I believed.

I left angry. I'm not angry anymore. After years of struggling with the nativity miracle, I finally decided that if God can create the universe, he can give his son a human body in whatever way he wants, even if that means being born of a virgin.

I will never fully comprehend the mystery of the incarnation or any of the other great mysteries of the faith. But I can, like a child, simply believe them. When I confront a mystery and find myself unable to explain it, then I am closest to God. If I can explain God and define him and put him in a nice package, then I have not discovered him at all. He's much bigger than any package I can come up with.

My prayer now is that he would restore to me the childlike wonder that surely I must have once had, like my granddaughter Elly still has. I want God to let me look at a rock with curiosity and wonder, and then ask, "Why is this rock so beautiful?" It's in such a moment that I am discovering God as a little child and dancing. And *it's never too late to dance.*

Dance Steps — Questions For Reflection

1. Relate, if you can, an opportunity you had helping a child become aware of God. Did either of you come away from it dancing, that is, rejoicing?
2. When did you have a "Wow!" moment in your spiritual journey that left your heart dancing?
3. Were you more open to discovering God and his Son Jesus Christ when you were younger or when you were older? What, if anything, has changed for you?
4. Where do you feel closer to God, by yourself in prayer and meditation, with others in a church gathering, or out in nature? Why?
5. How can your experience of God in all these ways be complementary, that is, how can each inform and enhance the other?
6. How comfortable are you around people who have had experiences of God in ways different from yours? Do you feel a need to correct or to encourage them? Why?
7. Do you prefer a traditional or contemporary church or no church at all? Why?
8. What have you discovered about God away from church that you never experienced in a class or sitting in the pew?
9. How difficult is it for you to talk with dying people, especially loved ones, about end of life issues? Why?
10. If you have experienced a miracle or vision, how has it affected your faith? Has it drawn you closer to God and his Son Jesus Christ, or pulled you toward something different?
11. How comfortable are you with questions for which there seem to be no answers? Can you dance with uncertainty? Why or why not?

The Sixth Dance Step To Joy — Dance With Every Success!

"When he had spit on the man's eyes and put his hands on him, Jesus asked, 'Do you see anything?' He looked up and said, 'I see people; they look like trees walking around.' Once more Jesus put his hands on the man's eyes. Then his eyes were opened, his sight was restored, and he saw everything clearly." Mark 8:23b-25

It was years ago when I was in junior high school — that's what they used to call it before it became "middle school." Mrs. Griffin, my Spanish teacher, was handing back our graded assignments. As she came to my desk, she looked at my paper briefly and then handed it to me. Eagerly I took it. A big capital letter "C" was scrawled in red across the top of the page.

"C? How did I get a C?" I asked indignantly. "I studied hard for this!"

"It just wasn't very good," she explained.

"But I did my best!" I argued.

Mrs. Griffin was not impressed. She raised her voice, addressing not just me but the whole class, "Your best is not good enough!"

After that little exchange, I decided I didn't like Spanish, and for the rest of the semester I didn't bother working very hard. Why should I? No matter how much effort I put into it, I would never please Mrs. Griffin. My best would never be good enough.

It was a powerful message. Mrs. Griffin did more than teach me Spanish. She taught me that unless my efforts resulted in perfection, I was a failure. I was a hopeless case. I might as well forget Spanish since I would never master the language. And for that matter, I shouldn't bother trying to learn anything else unless there was some likelihood I would do it perfectly.

If you and I choose to accept such impossible standards, we're not going to have many successes to dance with, by that I mean opportunities for joy. But even Jesus — whom the Bible teaches was without sin — didn't always get it right the first time. On at least one occasion, it took Jesus two attempts. Here's the story:

...some people brought a blind man and begged Jesus to touch him. He took the blind man by the hand and led him outside the village. When he had spit on the man's eyes and put his hands on him, Jesus asked, "Do you see anything?" He looked up and said, "I see people; they look like trees walking around." Once more Jesus put his hands on the man's eyes. Then his eyes were opened, his sight was restored, and he saw everything clearly... (Mark 8:22-25 NRSV).

I am not suggesting that this story implies sin or imperfection in the person of Jesus. He is always the holy Son of God. But he was also a human being just as we are, and as a human being, he grew and learned just as we do. In fact, the Bible says that as a boy, "Jesus grew in wisdom and stature, and in favor with God and man" (Luke 2:52). I take that to mean Jesus didn't exit the womb of Mary a master carpenter or an accomplished teacher. He probably hit his finger with a hammer a few times before he could drive a nail straight. Maybe he took a wrong turn on a teaching and healing mission once or twice.

Holiness and perfection of human nature are very different from growth and development as human beings. By faith in Christ, God considers us his holy and perfect children. But it's still going to take some hard work and practice for us to get good at certain things. Maybe we'll never master something like — say, playing the organ like E. Power Biggs, or the violin like Jascha Heifetz, or speaking Spanish like a native — but we can become adequate. And when we have even the smallest success after applying ourselves, it's worth a celebration, it's worth dancing over.

Whether we're young adults just beginning life's journey, or much farther along, it's never too late to dance. All it takes is realizing that demanding perfection of ourselves is just totally unrealistic. Instead, whenever we achieve any measure of progress at all, when we see any improvement in a small or big way, in a talent we're trying to learn or a behavior we're trying to change, we celebrate it. Dancing is what happens when we celebrate every success.

Perhaps you remember the spiritual gifts movement in the 1970s. Inspired by such teachers as Ray Stedman and C. Peter Wagner, Christians of every stripe began pouring over Bible study materials and checklists trying to figure out what special gifts, talents and abilities they'd been given by the Holy Spirit. When we discovered our "gifts," we were supposed to develop them and use them for the benefit of the church.

Saint Paul provides several groupings of such gifts that formed the basis for the lists we worked with. For example, in Romans, Paul includes gifts of prophesying, serving, teaching, encouraging, giving, leading, and showing mercy (Romans 12:6-8). In his first letter to the church at Corinth Paul mentions wisdom, knowledge, faith, healing, miracles, distinguishing between spirits, and different kinds of tongues (1 Corinthians 12:8-10). Another list is found in the Ephesians letter, where Paul says Christ has gifted the church with apostles, prophets, pastors and teachers to equip God's people for works of service (Ephesians 4:11-12).

Pentecostal churches have always encouraged the discovery and use of all these gifts. Other churches, especially mainline Protestants, have generally discouraged the use of speaking in tongues and prophesying or recognizing new apostles. The idea is that these were temporary gifts given by the Spirit to the church in the early years, enabling its initial establishment, but they are no longer needed. The debate still goes on.

So why bring up this matter of spiritual gifts? In the 1970s when all the excitement was being churned up, church members were using their spiritual gifts checklists as excuses for not doing certain things in the congregation. For example, if you had worked your way through a Bible study and filled out your gifts inventory, maybe you discovered you had the gift of encouragement but not the gifts of teaching or giving. Thus, when it came time to filling the roster of Sunday school teachers, you felt no sense of duty to volunteer.

Or when the annual stewardship drive was held, you felt no need to increase your pledge because you didn't have the gift of giving. So rather than helping the church, the movement in some ways actually had a dampening effect.

One of my professors at Denver Seminary, Dr. Kermit Ecklebarger, offered some helpful correctives to all this. While not denying that some people were amazingly gifted by the Holy Spirit in certain areas, that in no way relieved the rest of us from working in those areas too. Some pastors were gifted evangelists, he pointed out. Droves of people would be converted and added to the church under their ministry. But the rest of us who were not gifted evangelists were not thereby relieved from doing the work of an evangelist. The fruit of our labors might be less bountiful, but we were nonetheless called to evangelize. "You may never be gifted at some things," Dr. Ecklebarger said, "but you can at least become adequate."

You can at least become adequate. That told me I didn't have to be perfect. It told me that my best was indeed good enough. I could be like the state of Oklahoma's motto, "Oklahoma is okay." It's not a perfect state, but it's "okay." So, whether gifted or not, there is much that we do simply because it needs to be done. "Okay" works. The results may not be perfect, but it gets done. And when it gets done it's a small success worth celebrating, worth dancing over.

My wife once decided to wax the car. She'd been asking me to do it. The hot sun in our clear New Mexico sky is murder on automobile finishes. Regular waxing helps the paint last longer. But I procrastinated and she got tired of nagging me.

So, one day Kathy said, "I'm going outside to wax the car." An hour later she came in and announced, "It's done."

"You're done?" I asked, incredulous.

When I wax a car, it takes all day, but that's because my goal is perfection. I go over every square inch of sheet metal multiple times and wipe off every trace of haze. In the cracks I use Q-tips. My obsession with perfection is also why I so seldom do it. So, when Kathy said, "It's done," I was horrified. I was sure I would have to do it all over again. But I didn't. If I had, she would have been insulted. If I had wanted it done perfectly, I could have done it myself. So instead, I just went outside and admired Kathy's work and allowed her a moment of joy. She could celebrate her success with dancing.

This idea of celebrating the smallest success or moral improvement doesn't work in Pauline theology as it relates to human nature. Saint Paul had no room at all for anything short of total perfection. But he made it clear that was not possible:"As it is written, 'There is none righteous, no, not one...,'" Paul said, quoting Isaiah in his letter to the Romans, and, "For all have sinned, and come short of the glory of God..." (Romans 3:10, 23).

He reminds me of Mrs. Griffin. If there's no chance that my best is going to be even slightly pleasing to God, I might as well quit trying. And that's exactly the effect Saint Paul hopes his words will have. He wants to demolish any hope of sinners trying to perfect their fallen human nature through their own efforts, so that they will instead flee to Christ and his cross for mercy.

Thus, after each statement of our hopeless condition, Paul proclaims our only hope is believing that, "a person is justified by faith apart from the works of the law" (Romans 3:28), and "it is by grace you have been saved, through faith — and this is not from yourselves, it is the gift of God" (Ephesians 2:8), and "God made you alive with Christ. He forgave us all our sins" (Colossians 2:13).

Unfortunately, many people who attend church only hear Saint Paul's bad news about our sinful imperfection. Maybe some preachers just don't make clear the complementary good news of the gospel that offers forgiveness and God's mercy in Christ. Convinced that they can never please God, that they can never improve, and that no effort on their part holds any prospect of moving God to look on them favorably, some people just throw in the towel. They drop out of church altogether.

On the other hand, there are those who hear the demands of God's law, think they've done a surprisingly good job of keeping it, and come off feeling quite proud of themselves. That, of course, is Pharisaic. And that definitely is not something the New Testament views favorably.

Once a wealthy young man, probably a Pharisee, asked Jesus, "Good teacher, what must I do to inherit eternal life?"

Jesus answered him, "You know the commandments: 'You shall not commit adultery, you shall not murder, you shall not steal, you shall not give false testimony, honor your father and mother.'"

"All these I have kept since I was a boy," the young man replied.

When Jesus heard this, he said to him, "You still lack one thing. Sell everything you have and give to the poor, and you will have treasure in heaven. Then come, follow me."

When he heard this, we're told that the young man became very sad, because he was very wealthy (Luke 18:18-23).

You'll notice that when Jesus hit the one area the young man was less than perfect in, *generosity*, the air went out of his balloon. Jesus' intent here, just it was for Saint Paul in Romans, was to knock any sense of self-righteousness out of this young man and get him humbly to admit even he needed God's grace and forgiveness. He may have gotten the message but he did not go away dancing. Apparently, he was unwilling to embrace the free gift of forgiveness Jesus was there to offer him if it meant sharing his wealth.

So, given that everyone is less than perfect, and before God we have nothing to boast about, how do we still dance with our little successes and accomplishments, big or small? First, we recognize that we're dealing with two different areas of perfection. One area is the human heart. The other is the area of our everyday accomplishments.

The human heart is less than perfect. Both the Bible and our conscience teach us that. We've all sinned. But the gospel tells us that, by faith, our guilt is taken away and borne by Jesus to the cross. In place of our guilt God freely grants us forgiveness and righteousness. "The old has gone, the new has come," says Saint Paul. Christians see themselves as God's word says we are, "a new creation" (2 Corinthians 5:17). That is our new and present reality in the kingdom of God.

Then, as a new creation in God's eyes, perfect and holy by faith in Christ, we go about our daily tasks in this world with a joyful new freedom. Since Jesus has already been perfect for us, we don't have to be perfect at anything. Even as a parent is pleased and delighted with the efforts of his children, so also God is pleased and delighted with us.

I remember as a child in elementary school I made a crude ceramic dish for my grandmother. It was lumpy, the green glaze was not evenly distributed, and there were rough edges here and there. It was really quite ugly. But I gave it to my grandmother and she loved it. She loved it not because of its perfection but because she loved me. My gift moved her heart to dancing, and it moved my heart to dancing because she so graciously accepted it.

God loves us and delights in us even when we fail miserably. Hopefully we can remember that as we are struggle with the many social evils we succumb to these days. I have in mind the plague of addictions that have descended on our culture like a dark cloud; alcohol, drugs, promiscuity, gambling. Christian people are afflicted with these demons just as readily as non-Christians. Whether we are believers or not, when we're trapped in the addiction cycle, feelings of worthlessness and guilt overwhelm us.

We hate these feelings. We hate the problems these addictions lead to at our workplace, in our family life, in our health, in our relationship with God. We resolve never again to do this or that, and we apologize to those we have hurt, and maybe we go to counseling or join a support group. "I'm going to defeat this demon!" we tell ourselves. And for a while, maybe we have some success. We go for a day, or a week, or maybe a month without slipping up. We start feeling better about ourselves. We allow ourselves to start dancing again, first with hesitating step, then with gusto.

And then suddenly we crash. Things happen, temptations arise, and we fall right back into what we were doing. The familiar feelings of guilt and self-loathing come roaring back and with them a sense of despair. Where did that sense of despair come from? It came from all those Mrs. Griffins in our lives who taught us that our best was not good enough and that we had to be perfect and that if we weren't perfect, we were failures.

But that's not true! Every little success is worth celebrating with dancing. If I have an alcohol addiction, but with hard work, with treatment and with the support of caring people in my life I make some progress, that's worth celebrating! If, for example, my pattern has been to get drunk every night, but I manage to make it a week before I get drunk the next time, that's progress! That's worth celebrating! That's worth dancing a jig over! Then, if I slip back, I accept it, forgive myself, remember that God still loves me, and then I try to make it for a week and a half of sobriety next time. And when I succeed, I celebrate with dancing again. And so on until I'm finally free.

Beating oneself up with guilt over one's lack of perfection doesn't fix anything. It just makes it more likely we'll stay beaten down. But celebrating every little success is fun, it's exhilarating, and it makes it more likely we'll keep having more successes. With every little success, we'll have increased joy, and we'll have more reasons to dance.

Personally, I've never had to struggle with drugs or alcohol — they just aren't a temptation for me. My problems have been in other areas, like coming across as being negative. A "Debbie Downer" is the term I heard someone use once. I remember attending an elders' meeting and having the chairman scold me for my lack of joy. According to Saint Paul, joy is a fruit of the Spirit along with love, peace, patience, kindness, goodness, faithfulness, gentleness, and self-control (Ephesians 5:22-23a). We all bear this spiritual fruit to one degree or another. I guess my fruit basket seemed pretty light on joy to the elder chairman.

He was probably right, but scolding me for it was not going to suddenly set my heart to dancing. It's like that sign I saw on an office wall, "The floggings will continue until morale improves." Right or wrong, I chose to let his criticism make me feel angry and that made me feel even less joyful and less like dancing.

Today I hope I would react differently. Hopefully I would recognize that my fruit basket was full of other things like patience and gentleness and thank God for that. And then, since the Spirit is the giver of joy, hopefully I would ask him to open my eyes widely to all the things in my life that give me joy; my grandchildren, for instance. Then, as I become more mindful of the good things, I'd feel more like rejoicing, my heart would dance more, and people like that elder chairman would see the change.

After all, it's hard to keep from smiling when you're feeling happy. Smiling is a sign that you're inwardly dancing. When others notice, they say something like, "My, you seem happy today!" and that confirms your progress and that in turn becomes one more reason for dancing.

Little successes and progress in any area of our lives are worth dancing over. A few years ago, I was helping my four-year-old grandson Ethan draw letters of the alphabet. Some letters were recognizable. Others weren't quite right. I showed him how to draw a capital letter "A" and he would draw his letter "A" right beside mine. But for some reason the two legs on his "A" were parallel lines. He couldn't seem to bring them together in a point at the top of the letter. Over and over, he tried and failed. After a few attempts he got discouraged and put his head down on the table.

I remember telling him, "That's okay, Ethan. Just be patient with yourself." I pointed out that his letter "E" was wonderful, and so was his letter "T." So rather than give up, convinced he'd never get his "A" right, he should celebrate the wonderful job he did on his "E" and "T." He could dance with those letters. Eventually he'd have a very presentable "A" if he didn't think he had to do one perfectly now. And of course, that's exactly what happened.

It's never too late to start celebrating the little successes, those bits of progress we make. You and I are new creatures in Christ whom God is absolutely delighted with. We have no reason to beat ourselves up over our lack of perfection. All our successes are delightful to God. He celebrates them because he loves us. And just as he celebrates, we can celebrate each little success too. In Christ, a "B" grade is an "A+." If you know and believe that, you can start dancing today. It's never too late to dance.

Dance Steps — Questions For Reflection

1. Are you satisfied with "okay" or does everything about you have to be perfect? Why?
2. How might demanding perfection of yourself be a recipe for pain and failure?
3. What successes, small or large, have you had that you're especially proud of?
4. Who in your life has been difficult or impossible to please? How have you dealt with it?
5. Do you see God more as a demanding school master or as an encouraging friend? How is he both in the Bible? Which gives you a dancing heart?
6. How do you reconcile Jesus' two attempts at healing a blind man with the Bible's teaching that he is the sinless Son of God?
7. If you have small children or grandchildren, what homemade gifts have they given you? How did their gifts make you feel?
8. How does God view our flawed gifts of service and love to him? What role does the gospel play in this?
9. If you are fighting an addiction, do you see God as your cheerleader or judge? How can you dance even if you have relapses?
10. Name something you want to do but have been discouraged from attempting because you were afraid you wouldn't do it perfectly. What will you tell yourself to encourage you to try?
11. Whom can you encourage to try something new? How will you help them find confidence?

The Seventh Dance Step To Joy — Dance With Contentment!

"I have learned in whatever situation I am to be content."
Philippians 4: 11b

I've always liked folk music. It tells the story of human nature — our highest aspirations as well as our shameful flaws. Folk music often calls us to something else; peace instead of war, love instead of hate, equality instead of discrimination, moving on instead of staying put.

A group popular in the 1960s was The New Christy Minstrels. They disbanded in the 1970s but they've regrouped again. Once more, they're so popular that when they perform every concert is sold out. So, if you want to attend a show, get your tickets early.

One of the New Christy Minstrels' hits was "Green, Green," written by Randy Sparks, the group's leader. The refrain spoke of how things seem greener or better somewhere else. It spoke of going somewhere else to ease the discontent.[12] Please go online and listen to the words.

Do remember that song? That song was at the top of the charts for months in 1963. If you did ever hear it, you can probably still sing it.

"Green, Green" is a song that speaks to our inclination toward being discontent, unhappy with our circumstances. We always want something better than what we've got. When whatever we've got or whatever we're doing for a living or whoever our spouse is never seems to be good enough, that's discontentment. And when we're discontent, we're not happy. We're miserable and miserable people are not dancing.

But it's never too late to dance, right? All that's needed is a change in our negative way of thinking. And when we change the way we think, our emotions change. And when our emotions

12 Randy Sparks, New Christy Minstrels, song lyrics, "Green, Green" (New York: Columbia, Division of SonyMusic Entertainment, 1963).

change, so does our behavior. We discover ourselves capable of living grateful, happy lives. When I renounce discontentment and determine to be happy, whatever my circumstances, I cease being a wallflower and move back onto the dance floor of life. Contentment is a key to dancing once again.

I maintain that the root cause of most unhappiness in our world is choosing not to be content. There's something about human nature that inclines us to think we always need something more, that we deserve something better. And until we get it, we have a right to be resentful and feel miserable. So, that's how we choose to feel. But how much do we really need? And how much of our discontentment is really just greed and unthankfulness?

I'd like to share with you some statistics. These come from the World Bank. In 2013, 10.7 % of the world's population lived on less than $1.90 a day. Million of theses were children! Could you live on $1.90 a day? Maybe some Americans do, but most of us don't, not even the poorest among us.[13]

I'm sure you've heard of Jeff Foxworthy and his "You might be a redneck" jokes. Here's a sample: "If you cut your grass and find a car, you might be a redneck." Or this one, "If your dog and your wallet are both on a chain, you might be a redneck."[14]

Well, here's a takeoff from Jeff Foxworthy but it's not funny. It's a list of "You might be rich" statements that apply to a huge chunk of the world's population. To 767 million people:

You might be rich if you have more than one pair of shoes.

You might be rich if you can choose what clothes to put on today.

You might be rich if you don't have to sleep outside.

You might be rich if you have clean water to drink whenever you want it.

You might be rich if at least once a day you have something to eat.

You might be rich if you can read.

13 World Bank Poverty Statistics, (Washington, D.C.:www.worldbank.org, 2013).

14 Jeff Foxworthy, in Henno Kruger, "30 of the Best Jeff Foxworthy You-Might-Be-a-Redneck Jokes"(https://rwrant.co.za/jeff-foxworthy-you-might-be-a-redneck-quotes/).

You might be rich if you're a kid who can say, "When I grow up" rather than "If I grow up."

Speaking for myself, there's never been a time in my life that I've not been far better off than anyone who would consider himself rich by those standards. I've always had plenty to dance about, but I haven't always been dancing. How about you? If we haven't always been content, it's not something new. It's a problem as old as humanity. As I page through the Bible, discontentment seems to be a common theme:

Adam and Eve were discontent when God didn't allow them to eat from the tree of the knowledge of good and evil. All the other fruit in the garden was theirs, whatever they wanted, but that wasn't good enough. So, they gave in to temptation, ate the forbidden fruit, and brought sin, suffering and death into the world (Genesis 3).

Jacob was discontent when his older brother Esau was to receive the family blessing and inheritance from their father Isaac. Jacob tricked Isaac into blessing him, thus stealing the blessing from Esau. Esau became so enraged when he found this out he planned to kill Jacob. Jacob was forced to run for his life, spending the next few decades living in fear of his brother (Genesis 27-28ff).

The Israelites were discontent with Moses even though he led them out of slavery in Egypt to freedom in the desert. Under his leadership, they had water from the rock to drink when they grew thirsty and every day they had manna to eat they picked up off the ground. But it wasn't the same as the leeks and melons and pots of meat and bread they were accustomed to. So, they complained bitterly against God and Moses (Exodus 15-17).

This ongoing discontentment of Israel is wrapped in, under and around every one of the Ten Commandments Moses later brought down from Mount Sinai. God's anger with his people's discontentment seems to be bubbling and seething beneath the surface in every line of the decalogue. Consider this:

"You shall have no other God's before me" (Exodus 20:3). Israel didn't live in a vacuum. There were different cultures all around them that honored gods different from their God, Yahweh. When things weren't going well, the Israelites were often tempted to turn away from Yahweh to these other gods that seemed to offer something better. That's discontentment.

"Remember the sabbath day and keep it holy" (Exodus 20:8). Setting aside the seventh day of the week for rest distinguished Israel from its neighbors. Even so, merchants were irritated when they showed up at the gates of an Israelite town on the sabbath to do business only to discover the gates closed. Why? Because losing a day's work meant losing a day's profits. Less money meant discontentment.

"Honor your father and your mother" (Exodus 20:12). Why would a kid need to hear that? Because parents are the gatekeepers for what their kids want. When parents don't let kids have what they want, usually it's because parents know what's best for them. But kids don't like it and get resentful. That's discontentment.

Once when I was little and didn't get my way with my Dad, I remember telling him, "I hate you! I'm going to throw you down the sewer!" I don't know how I thought a six-year-old was going to throw a 200-pound man down the sewer, but that's what I said. I'm surprised I lived to tell you about it. I was angry. I was discontent.

Whenever discontentment leads us to break a commandment, we always break at least three. We dishonor God in order to bow to some idol. We dishonor our parents in order take something that isn't ours: someone's life, someone's spouse, someone's reputation, and so on. Even wanting to break a commandment involves coveting and coveting is discontentment.

That's the way it is when we violate God's law. We can't murder, commit adultery, steal, bear false witness, or covet without both denying God and dishonoring our parents. So, if you think you broke one commandment, you probably really broke a bunch of them.

Here's what I mean: Does murder please God and honor our parents? Does adultery please God and honor our parents? Does stealing or telling lies please God and honor our parents? Of course not! There's no way we can murder or hate someone and have God say, "Well done, good and faithful servant!" (Matthew 25:23). There's no way we can rob our neighbor or tell lies about him and have our parents say, "I'm so proud of you!" Maybe there are a few parents so morally and spiritually sick they would say that, perhaps someone like a character out of a Charles Dickens novel, but no normal parent would.

The point is that all ten of the commandments speak to our inclination to be discontent. Their purpose is to make us aware of that tendency so that when we finally admit to being ungrateful and discontent we can repent. And when we do repent — adopting and practicing God's values as reflected in his law of love — we're happy! We don't feel like brooding and sulking any more. Instead, we feel like, well, dancing!

So, what does repentance look like? Repentance is changing one's mind about something and as a result, changing one's direction. Thus, if I discover myself to be a greedy person, that I'm selfishly unwilling to share my abundance, I change my mind about that. I decide that my greed is not a good thing, that it's not pleasing to God, that it doesn't help my neighbor, that it gives me a guilty conscience. So, I resolve to change my thinking and my behavior.

Then I adopt a new approach to my money and my stuff, my time and my talent. From now on, I resolve to be a generous person and share what I have. And that's what I do. If you're familiar with Charles Dickens' *A Christmas Carol*, you know that's what Scrooge does after being visited by ghosts in a dream. The old skinflint becomes a benevolent employer who buys a fat goose for his impoverished clerk, Bob Crachett.[15]

But a change in one's behavior isn't all that repentances involves. Along with a change of heart and mind and direction, real repentance involves turning in faith to Christ who loves me and graciously forgives me. He then becomes the model for my new values and my new direction in life.

It might be helpful to know what repentance is not. There's a lot of phony repentance going around these days. Phony repentance is being sorry I got caught, but not that I've actually done or thought something wrong. Phony repentance is saying something like, "I'm sorry if I offended you," rather than saying, "I'm sorry I hurt you." Phony repentance is being sorry for my

15 Charles Dicken, *A Christmas Carol in Pros Being a Ghost Story of Christmas* (London: Chapman and Hall, 1843).

greedy or otherwise bad behavior — maybe even crying — but not being sorry enough to change it.

Phony repentance is what I heard a politician say once. He didn't use these exact words but, essentially, he said, "I didn't do anything wrong and I promise never to do it again." Another one said, "I take full responsibility for the actions of my department," without actually admitting anything she'd done wrong. In fact, she just blamed the people who worked for her. She was responsible but she refused to be held personally accountable. That's phony repentance.

If we want to see real repentance in action we can look to the New Testament and the preaching of John the Baptist. John the Baptist was not your usual kind of religious leader. He was not clergy, although he was the son of a priest. In fact, he seems to have intentionally avoided the inherited job of priest in order to assume the role of unpaid and independent prophet.

Accountable only to God and his own conscience, John's goal in preaching was to rearrange the hearts and thoughts of his hearers and bring about changed behavior. He sought to move people away from sin and direct them to Jesus Christ, the one whom he proclaimed to be "the Lamb of God who takes away the sins of the world" (John 1:29).

The Bible describes the droves of people who came out from Jerusalem and the towns of Judah to hear John preaching in the desert by the Jordan River. A few groups in particular who came to John for baptism are pointed out. To these, John prescribed personalized repentance plans. What might a personalized repentance plan look like for you? Here's what personalized repentance looked like for John's audience:

For Pharisees and Sadducees, a personalized repentance plan meant they were to stop bragging about their descent from Abraham and start bearing good fruit in keeping with repentance (Matthew 3:7). How many of us brag about our ethnicity or theological pedigree?

For people who had more than one change of clothes and extra food, a personalized repentance plan meant sharing their abundance with those in need. Today, that would apply to just about anyone living on more than $1.90 a day. I'm thinking that includes anyone reading this.

For tax collectors a personalized repentance plan meant collecting no more than they were authorized to. If John were here, he might be telling you and me that as taxpayers we're to pay what the law requires. Many of us these days do business under the table to avoid paying taxes. Do you? If you're a small business person, do you pay your gross receipts tax? If you have a housekeeper, do you pay the employer's part of her social security contribution?

For soldiers, a personalized repentance plan meant they were not to extort money from anyone but rather "be content with your wages" (Matthew 3:10-14). How many of us, discontent with our wages, have dipped into the till at work or grabbed something off the shelf when we thought no one was looking, just because we thought we deserved it?

John knew that repentant people are changed people. When that change happens, and when our repentance meets God's forgiveness in Christ, our hearts become content. Greed and avarice are replaced with a joyful harvest of good fruit in our lives. And that, in turn, leads to happy hearts filled with dancing. Do you remember the story of Zacchaeus the tax collector? Here it is:

[Jesus] entered Jericho and was passing through. And behold, there was a man named Zacchaeus. He was a chief tax collector and was rich. And he was seeking to see who Jesus was, but on account of the crowd he could not, because he was small in stature. So he ran on ahead and climbed up into a sycamore tree to see him, for he was about to pass that way. And when Jesus came to the place, he looked up and said to him, "Zacchaeus, hurry and come down, for I must stay at your house today." So he hurried and came down and received him joyfully. And when they saw it, they all grumbled, "He has gone in to be the guest of a man who is a sinner." And Zacchaeus stood and said to the Lord, "Behold, Lord, the half of my goods I give to the poor.

*And if I have defrauded anyone of anything, I restore it fourfold." And
Jesus said to him, "Today salvation has come to this house, since he
also is a son of Abraham. For the Son of Man came to seek and to save
the lost." (Luke 19:1-10)*

This is the story of a greedy man who had hurt many but who
now truly repented. How do we know this was real repentance
and not phony repentance? We know because Zacchaeus does
the kind of thing repentant people do. He gives half his goods
to the poor. He pays back anyone he defrauded four times over.
And he receives Jesus joyfully into his home. His Scrooge-like
heart is completely transformed. Perhaps late in life, he discovers
happiness and learns to dance.

Let me share with you a true story of contentment. Ysleta
Lutheran Mission in El Paso hosts many groups throughout the
year who use it as home base. People from churches all over
the country stay at the mission, which they use as their point of
departure for doing cross-border human care projects. Sometimes
they come with tractor trailers loaded with all the materials they
need and build houses for very poor people in Mexico. Maria,
who lives in Juarez, would cross the border into Texas regularly
to cook for these workers at the mission. Like the visiting builders,
she wanted to help the poor people.

One day Maria finished her work late. It wasn't safe for her to
go home alone so one of the staff members asked if she could give
Maria a ride home. Maria looked alarmed. She didn't want a ride
home. The staff member persisted and Maria finally agreed. But
rather than let the staff member take her all the way home, she
wanted to be dropped off a few blocks from where she lived. That
wasn't safe either so despite Maria's protests the staff member
took Maria all the way home. That's when it was discovered that
Maria lived in shack just like the people for whom the mission
workers were building houses.

In all the years Maria cooked for these groups, she never let
on that she lived in a shack too. All she said was she wanted to
cook for the volunteers so they could "build houses for the poor
people." Never did she ask for a house for herself! She thought
she had what she needed and other people had greater needs.

When volunteers from Colorado learned the truth, they built a house for Maria. Maria had been content and danced with her blessings even before she had her own new house. Now Maria dances with contentment, shares her new one room house with her whole family and is a leader in her church.

Saint Paul said, "I have learned in whatever situation I am to be content" (Philippians 4: 11b). Paul was in prison when he wrote that. Thankfulness was the secret he had discovered. His letters from prison are overflowing with thankfulness for people who loved him. Knowing he was loved, Paul could be content anywhere.

Could you and I be content in prison? Could we be content if we were living in a shack? Have we learned the secret of being content? When we have, we're happy, as happy as Saint Paul or as happy as Maria. Whatever our situation, when generosity, gratitude, and contentment fill our hearts, we dance with joy. And it's never too late to dance!

Dance Steps — Questions For Reflection

1. When have you and your family been most content, in hard times or lean? Explain.
2. Tell about a time in your life when you were in need. How did you get through it? What gave you joy?
3. When has greed gotten you in trouble? What lessons did you learn?
4. Which of the Ten Commandments is hardest for you to keep? Why?
5. How will you overcome discontentment in this area?
6. Do you see repentance as a one-time event or a life-long challenge?
7. What's the toughest apology you've ever had to make? Or do you still need to make it? Why is making an apology so hard?
8. If John the Baptist were to prescribe for you a personal repentance plan, what would it include?
9. In what areas of your life are you most discontent? In what areas are you most content?
10. What are the top ten blessings in your life right now?
11. How would your thinking have to change for you to start dancing with contentment today?

The Eighth Dance Step To Joy — Dance With Your Work!

"Everyone should eat and drink and take pleasure in all his toil — this is God's gift to man." Ecclesiastes 3:13

I was at an office supply store the other day waiting for the copier to finish printing a project I had brought in. A display of greeting cards caught my eye. There were the usual ones you'd expect to find — birthday greetings, best wishes for those moving on, congratulations on promotions, and the like. And then there was this one for someone who didn't like his job. I had to have it, so I bought it.

The front of the card starts with "Sorry to hear that your job..." And then there's a list of options. The recipient is told to "Check all that apply." The whole thing reads like this, "Sorry to hear that your job:

__ sucks.
__ is hard.
__ is thankless.
__ pays poorly.
__ requires regular attendance.
__ eats into your free time.
__ gives you the heebie-jeebies.
__ puts you into a boredom-induced coma.
__ saps your soul.
__ is slowly driving you insane.
__ makes you wonder if violence really is the answer.
__ could be performed by a monkey."

When you open the card up, the inside says, "On a positive note:

__ 'unemployed' doesn't look as impressive on a resume
__ there is the whole paycheck thing
__ [and] some monkeys make great pets."[16]

16 Greeting Card from *Whip-SMART* (Stillwater, MN: Gartner Greetings Inc., undated).

Who of us hasn't complained about his job? We all do it, don't we? But work is a huge part of life. Maybe our job isn't particularly glamorous or exciting or high paying, but if we've got a job, any job, it's better than no job. And work is a gift from God. His will for us, as observed by King Solomon, is that we "take pleasure in all our toil," or put another way, that we dance with our work.

Ecclesiastes is one of those books in the Bible that leaves us scratching our heads and asking, "Why in the world is this depressing book in here?" Solomon, probably an old man when he wrote it, seemed to say that just about everything human beings do or pursue in life is "vanity," "a chasing after the wind." That is, it's worthless, futile, or pointless.

Solomon spoke from experience. He had owned and done just about everything. If anyone had a right to wear a T-shirt that says, "Been there, done that," it was Solomon. He knew what he was talking about. He had spent his entire life pursuing pleasure, possessions, wisdom, and knowledge and concluded in the end that it was all vanity.

He owned vineyards, gardens, parks, fruit trees, and forests. He had slaves, herds, and flocks numbering in the thousands. His palaces were filled with hundreds of wives and concubines. He had all the gold and silver a king could want. His wealth was so vast, it would have rivaled Croesus, the ancient king of Lydia who, according to legend, had so much money he invented coins so he could keep track of it.

But, observed Solomon, in the end he would die just like everyone else and all his wealth would be dispersed. And who could tell whether his heirs would be wise or foolish? Our character, our accomplishments, all that we've accumulated, whatever we've valued in life — ultimately none of it matters, Solomon mused. Whether human or animal, every living creature eventually ends up dead and returns to the dust, to the soil from which it came. Isn't that a happy thought that just sets your heart to dancing?

Most of the book is like that, one depressing verse after another. But hidden in all that despair are some real gems of hope, truths that rescue us from despondency. When we discover these redemptive truths and embrace them as Solomon did, the despair goes away, vanity is replaced with purpose and meaning, and every day becomes an opportunity for dancing.

So, what are these truths? Two of them are found in the last chapter of Ecclesiastes where Solomon says, "Fear God and keep his commandments, for this is the whole duty of man" (12:13b). But the one we focus on today is, "everyone should eat and drink and take pleasure in all his toil," (3:13) or as Solomon says a bit later, "a man should rejoice in his work" (3:22).

Take pleasure in toil and rejoice in work? This is a dance step for a happy life? Absolutely! For a happy life, dance with your work! Think back to the creation story. In the first chapter of Genesis, the Creator gives human beings two prime directives, to use the language of Star Trek. What are they? Here's the first; "Be fruitful and multiply and fill the earth and subdue it" (1:28). We've done a pretty good job carrying out that directive. As of today, there are about 7.88 billion of us on the planet.[17]

The second prime directive is what we consider here. It's not specifically stated but it's implied. We're told in Genesis, chapter 2, that "The LORD God took the man and put him in the Garden of Eden to tend it and keep it" (2:15). Tending and keeping a garden — what would you call that? I'd call that work. And since sin doesn't enter the world until the Genesis 3, work was all joy, it was all dancing.

I haven't actually planted a garden for many years. But when I had one, despite the constant battle against weeds and bugs, gardening was fun. Turning over the soil, planting the seeds, watering, watching the plants grow — it was thoroughly rewarding! One summer I had squash that developed faster than I could pick it. I had okra plants that became huge bushes loaded with pods. My tomato vines were so heavy with fruit they lay on the ground. The tomatoes were so sweet I could eat them right there in the garden. And I did!

What joy that was! Wouldn't it be wonderful if all our work was that pleasant? If it were, we'd wake up early because we

17 World Population as of 5/20/2021, https://countrymeters.info

couldn't wait to get started on our day and it would be quitting time before we knew it.

That's the way it was for my wife Kathy and me when we were fixing up the old Mesilla Park farmhouse she inherited from her parents. We'd start work early in the morning. Hours later we'd realize we hadn't even taken time to eat. We were so "into" our work sometimes it would be one or two o'clock in the morning before we fell exhausted but happy into bed. We loved what we were doing! Those were some the happiest days of our marriage. Yes, it was hard and dirty work, but for Kathy and me it was our way of dancing.

Sadly, often we don't see our daily work that way. Often, we view our job as something that gets in the way of what we really want to do. A bumper sticker I saw once said, "Livin' for the weekend!" as though useful work got in the way of what life was really all about.

But thinking back to Genesis, is it God's intent that we work to live, or that we live to work? Remember those two directives he gave us, "Be fruitful and multiply," and "tend the garden and keep it." And of course, later on, in the decalogue, God says, "Six days you shall labor" (Exodus 20:9).

So, it would seem to me that what's most important for dancing, according to God's design, is family and work. And if work is part of God's intent — and it is — than we might as well figure out how to value it and enjoy it. We might as well learn how to dance joyfully with our work, whatever it might be.

And how do we do that? Well, first, dancing with our work begins with realizing that Jesus sanctifies and makes holy every wholesome job we undertake. Christians believe Jesus is the l Son of God through whom the Father made all things. "In the beginning, God created the heavens and the earth," the Bible tells us (Genesis 1:1). Saint John said God did his creative work through the pre-incarnate Christ whom he calls "the Word." "All things were made through him and without him was not anything made that was made," said John (John 1:3).

What would you call this act of creation? I'd call it work. It's toil. It's labor. But for God and Christ the Son, it was not a "necessary evil," as we might think of our job. Rather, it was exactly the opposite. It was a task God rejoiced in! How does the Bible describe God's work after he finished his work of creating? It says, "…and behold, it was very good" (Genesis 1:31).

The finished creation was God's temple, it was his throne room. And it was beautiful. That's how he wants us to see the place where we work, whether it's a church, a school, a hospital room, a shop floor, a kitchen, or a farm. That's the temple where we fulfill our calling, our vocation.

But when Adam decided he didn't like the arrangements God made with him, sin entered the world. Work became no longer a joy but a chore, a burden. It became toil and sweat, thorns and trouble. But work remains God's intention for us; it's still a good thing, a gift from God.

Partly to press that point home and help us once again rejoice in our work, God took on the form of a human being, a servant. In the person of Jesus Christ, God came to our workplace. He blessed and sanctified the ordinary things we do at work every day by sharing human chores and burdens.

I'm sure you remember Saint Joseph. He was the husband of Mary and the adoptive father of Jesus. What was Joseph's trade? He was a carpenter (Matthew 13:55). In Greek, the word is *tekton*. It can refer to an artisan, craftsman, woodworker or builder. A *tekton* is someone who makes things.

It's likely that Joseph plied his skills not in Nazareth where Jesus grew up, but in the nearby Roman town of Sepphoris. It was a new city still under construction. Lots of craftsmen were needed there and it was only a couple of miles from where the holy family lived. So, day after day, except on the sabbath, Joseph and young Jesus would probably have traveled there to work. Their labor would not have been easy.[18]

Can you imagine Jesus as a teenager chopping down trees, hewing logs into boards, sawing and shaping them, and nailing them into place? Can you imagine him breaking rocks with a hammer, chipping them smooth, and laying down a course of them for a wall? Can you imagine how rough Jesus' hands

18 Frontline, PBS TV program, "The Surprises of Sepphoris" (Boston: WGBH Educational Foundation, 1998).

must have been, how strong his arms and shoulders would have become, how brown he must have been from the hot sun? Can you imagine him at the end of each day, tired, his black hair matted and sticky with dried sweat and sawdust, and probably not smelling very good?

But it was the dance God sent Jesus to be part of — our dance. Every board he cut and every nail he drove, every splinter he got in his fingers and every rock he broke and carried — each task Jesus performed dignified and made sacred the work each of us does every day. His labor makes good and holy every job we do. It makes all our toil a sweet-smelling sacrifice acceptable to God, an offering worth dancing about.

Ultimately, it's not just work that we do, it's not just a job; it's a holy calling, a divine vocation. It's more than just leading the choir, doing payroll, cleaning up after vacation Bible school, teaching kids, or listening to a lonely person ramble on and on; it's a sacrifice of thanksgiving to God, blessed and made holy by our Lord Jesus. Thus, "Whether you eat or drink or whatever you do, do it all to the glory of God," said Saint Paul (1 Corinthians 10:31).

"Yes, but…" I can already hear the protests. Have you ever heard of a motorboat Christian? A motorboat Christian says, "But, but, but, but, but, but." You get the idea. We have lots of buts, lots of reasons why we think we have a right to hate our job and be resentful. Usually, they center on how awful and cheap and unfair our boss is, or how unkind and gossipy our co-workers are, or how rude and unappreciative people can be.

But dancing with our work, rejoicing in what we do, has nothing to do with our employer, or fellow workers, or the customers, or the church member in the pew, or any other working conditions. It has everything to do with the sacredness of the task, and the one for whom we really do it.

When the New Testament was written it's estimated that 35 to 40% of the Roman population in Italy were slaves. In the whole empire, about 10 to 15% were slaves for a total of over five million people. That means millions of people worked at tasks for which they were not paid, had no legal rights, had no power over their own bodies and could be killed by their owners at will. If you don't like your job today, think how slaves must have felt then.[19]

By the middle of the first century, many of these slaves were Christians and faithful members of the church. If you were a pastor in those days, how might you counsel a slave who was unhappy with his job? It might surprise you but here's what Saint Paul said:

> *Slaves, obey in everything those who are your earthly masters, not by way of eye-service, as people-pleasers, but with sincerity of heart, fearing the Lord. Whatever you do, work heartily, as for the Lord and not for men, knowing that from the Lord you will receive the inheritance as your reward. You are serving the Lord Christ.*
> (Colossians 3:22-24)

Did you catch Paul's secret for working happily, for dancing with your job, even if you feel like a slave? The key is realizing that the real Master for whom we are laboring is not the guy who cracks the whip or writes out the paycheck. The real Master is God himself and the Lord Jesus Christ. And serving our Lord through our daily labor is not a burden. It's a joy.

Jesus told us,

> *Come to me, all you who are weary and burdened, and I will give you rest. Take my yoke upon you and learn from me, for I am gentle and humble in heart, and you will find rest for your souls. For my yoke is easy and my burden is light.* (Matthew 11:28-30)

Jesus took upon himself a far more unpleasant job than we can ever imagine, the burden of carrying the weight all our sins to the cross. Wouldn't it be ironic if years before he had cut the very beams that became his own cross? We can't know that — I'm just speculating — but we do know that that the very trees that became his cross were created through his power. And it was though his labor that the work of the carpenter who made that cross was sanctified. And it was through Jesus' sacrifice on that cross that all our labor becomes a good and holy gift to God.

19 *Wikipedia: The Free Encyclopedia*, "Slavery in Ancient Rome" (San Francisco, CA, Los Angeles, CA and St. Petersburg, FL: Wikipedia Foundation, Inc., 2018).

The Eighth Dance Step

So, enjoy your work! Find pleasure in it! It's God's purpose for you! Embrace your work and dance with it as long as God gives you the strength. With every breath, may it bring dancing to your heart. And it's never too late to dance!

Dance Steps — Questions For Reflection

1. Would you rather go to work, stay home and watch TV, play sports, or go on a trip? Why?
2. When was the last time you said to yourself, "I love my job!"? What makes any job enjoyable for you? Or unenjoyable?
3. If you have a job you love, did you intentionally train for and seek it, or did you just stumble into it? What made you love it?
4. Do you see your work as something you do for yourself, your family, your boss, or God? Or all of the above? Explain.
5. If you could pick any job or career, what would it be? Or are you happy doing what you're already doing? Why?
6. How does knowing Jesus was a carpenter (craftsman) affect the way you feel about doing your work? Or does it have any effect?
7. What difference does realizing work is a way of bringing glory to God — that is, it's a way of worshiping him — make in the way you do your job?
8. How is your work and situation in life far better than being a slave? Or is it? What can you say to encourage yourself or someone else who says, "I hate my job"?
9. Suppose you are disabled, elderly or have poor health, what useful work can you still do that praises God and gives you joy?
10. The Bible says nothing about retirement. Since work is one our purposes in life, how will you use retirement to bring praise to God and dancing to your heart?
11. Some people speak of having a vocation and an avocation. A vocation is literally a "calling." An avocation is something you love to do that is not a calling. But how can every job be a calling?

The Ninth Dance Step To Joy — Dance With Your Past Into Your Future!

"…forgetting what lies behind and straining forward to what lies ahead, I press on toward the goal for the prize of the upward call of God in Christ Jesus." Philippians 3:13b-14

Variety shows were big on TV in the '60s and '70s. One popular host was Flip Wilson and especially his character "Reverend Leroy," minister of "The Church of What's Happenin' Now!" Who would want to go "The Church of What Happened Way Back When" when you could go to "The Church of What's Happenin' Now!"? It sounds a lot more exciting.

In one skit Reverend Leroy sent the deacons out to take up the collection. But the baskets came back empty. When the Reverend discovered this, he threw the deacons up against his pulpit like suspects against a police car and frisked them. Then he sent them back out into the congregation to take up the collection all over again.[20]

The Church of What's Happenin' Now! You'd think everyone would want to go there. You'd think all of us would want to live in the present and dance with the blessings God gives us today. But many of us don't. We get stuck in the past and don't seem to be able to move beyond it.

There's a Beatle's song that speaks of this fixation on the past. It speaks of how yesterday, or in the past, our troubles seemed far away, but they are now surfacing and a part of today. Listen to those words online. The song is titled "Yesterday".

I won't go through all the lyrics, but another verse speaks of love becoming more difficult and harder to face, so that it is easier to believe in the past.

Did you know that "Yesterday" is one of the most recorded songs in history? There are hundreds of versions of it out there.

20 *The Flip Wilson Show,* American TV variety show, National Broadcasting Company, 1970-1974.

It's been played millions and millions of times on radio and over the internet. People seem to like it even though the whole song is about the sadness of lost love.

We understand sadness and nostalgia, don't we? We get it. Sometimes we live in the past, thinking everything was so much better then. Or sometimes, we're stuck there wallowing in sorrow. Sometimes we let the pain and injustice we experienced long ago determine our present. Sometimes all we can do is recite our grievances over and over, clinging to them, unable to think about much of anything else. But when we're stuck in the past, whether it's good or bad, we're not dancing with our present or our future.

An elderly lady in Alamogordo, NM once asked me to come to her house to plan her funeral. All she wanted to talk about was her son and how badly he'd treated her years ago. She wasn't going to leave him anything in her will. She didn't even want him to attend her funeral, as if I had any control over that. There was no forgiveness, there was no love, there was no joy in her life. She was a Christian but she wasn't dancing. She was stuck in the past, fixated on something bad that happened between her and her son.

We've all been there, haven't we, stuck in the past over something? Maybe we're still there. Or, maybe we know someone who's there right now. When someone we know and love is stuck in the past, we get impatient with them. We tell them things like, "You really need to get over it," or "You really need to move on," or "You really need to let by bygones be bygones." And even if we don't tell them this, we say it to other people when we gossip about them or we say it to ourselves.

Yes, we do need to move beyond our pain! The longer we stay stuck in our past, the less we dance with our present and our tomorrow. We neglect those we love who are with us today. We forget how to dance with the joyful things that are happening now. When we're stuck in the past, how do we get back on the floor and dance into the present?

The key to getting back in the dance is taking an honest inventory of the past. Not everything that happened was good, nor was everything bad. No one we love who is now gone was as perfect as we imagine them to be. No one we dislike now was as bad as we think they were.

I facilitated a support group called "Survivors of Suicide Loss." The longer someone came to the group, the more I heard their story change over time. Soon after their loss, the one who had died was practically perfect, flawless. He or she was kind hearted, smart, loved by everyone, never did anything unkind, and so on.

But as the weeks went by, the grieving person started telling more of the story. Yes, their loved one had some great qualities but also some bad ones. Maybe a wife who took her life was difficult to live with. Maybe a daughter was strung out on drugs. Maybe a husband never listed his wife as the beneficiary on his pension plan and now as a widow she's getting nothing. So, the anger and the resentment over these things would start coming out. The perfect but lost loved one slowly became a villain.

But no one is either all good or all bad. Dancing with the past means coming to grips with that. Moving forward means we allow ourselves to see the imperfections in those we've lost as well as the things we loved about them.

The same thing is true of a marriage that ended in divorce. I've talked with people who are still filled with anger and resentment over a failed marriage and have nothing but bad things to say about their former spouse. But if the spouse was really all that evil, would they ever have gotten married in the first place? At least in the beginning, there was something good that each saw in the other. And surely something good remained even after the divorce.

Being able to dance with the past means becoming able to look at things soberly and honestly. We don't have to build up a false narrative to justify feeling whatever it is that we feel. We accept reality. We accept the bad. We rejoice in the good. We grieve the loss. And we dance hopefully into the new day, taking with us the scars that never go away but also the experiences that have made us better people.

Saint Paul did something like that. As he wrote his letter to the Philippian church, he was a Christian and an apostle, no longer the strict Pharisee he once was. He spoke about his former life, his family background, his Jewish religion, and his accomplishments. He mentioned the things he had been and had done that he's now ashamed of. Then he said he counted it all as loss. In fact he says it's "rubbish" — literally dung — compared to "the surpassing greatness of knowing Christ Jesus my Lord, ... not having a righteousness that comes from Law, but that which comes through faith in Christ" (Philippians 3:7-8).

You could get the impression that Saint Paul had tossed into the trash everything from his old pre-Christian life. But he hadn't, really. True, he trusted nothing from his past to save him — no Christian does — but he kept much of it. He still considered himself a Jew. He still maintained contact with his family and asked them for help occasionally. He still remained a Roman citizen and used the privileges of citizenship for his advantage when he could. And he continued to rely on his rabbinical training in theology and rhetoric. It showed up in his skills as a preacher and writer.

In fact, though Saint Paul no longer valued his old strict religious practices, much of what he believed before becoming a Christian showed up as doctrine in the New Testament. He believed in the same God he always did. He believed in God's love that had chosen and called him to eternal life. He believed in a spiritual world of angels who helped God's people and interacted with them. He believed in a judgment and resurrection of everyone on the last day. He had always believed these things.

What was different for Saint Paul after his conversion was that he now believed Jesus was the Christ, the Son of God sent by the Father to save sinners. And he believed that apart from faith in Christ, there was no other way to be saved.

Saint Paul remembered and clung to much that was true and good from his old life even while he chose to discard those things that were now useless baggage, or "rubbish" as he called it. What was this rubbish? It was his former belief that he was a good and holy person because of his Hebrew birth and heritage and that he was saved by keeping the ritual laws of Moses. All of that he tossed onto the trash pile for the sake of Christ that he might gain a righteousness that comes by faith.

As you and I recall our past — the traditions we've practiced, the people we've known and loved, ideas we've held — we realize that some of it's good and some of it isn't. Whatever was wholesome we continue to cherish, realizing it's helped make us who we are. What isn't good, we no longer cherish, even though it too has affected us. Good or bad, we don't stay stuck in the past. We move on, dancing into our present and on into our future.

Maybe you and I have some really bad memories. Maybe there's lingering sadness. Maybe we're still bitter about some things. Whichever it is, we don't let sadness or bitterness define us. We let our hope in Christ and the promises of the gospel change and define us. In doing so we rejoice — and we dance.

Three years ago, I joined my son Nathan and his new bride Cameron in holy matrimony. What a milestone in both their lives and in the lives of our families that backyard ceremony was! Five years ago, Nathan's first wife April took her life just before Christmas. How we all agonized and wept over her loss! In my mind, April was practically perfect. That's how I thought of her, even though I know she wasn't really. I didn't want to let April go. And I haven't. I still embrace all the good that was April. I still love April.

But now it's time to say "goodbye" to April's marriage to my son. She's gone and that marriage is over. So much healing has taken place as the months have passed. Nathan was ready for a new life with Cameron. My grandchildren Ellie and Mikey were ready for their new mother. It was time for me to leave behind my loss and sadness and dance into the joyful present with Nathan, Cameron, and my grandchildren.

Oh, it still hurts. I can still hardly believe April is gone. But she is, and nothing can change that. But there's a new reality that I and my family are finding joy in. Nathan is happy again. Cameron is happy. Her parents and sisters are happy. My grandkids are happy. I want to share in that happiness. I want to be there celebrating and dancing with all of them as long as I'm alive.

Maybe there'll be more grandchildren for Kathy and me to spoil. Maybe Nathan and his family will move away giving us a new place to visit. There are so many happy things to look forward to. I have a choice. I can just remain trapped in the fairy tale world of the past, brooding over the perfect family that never really existed, dumping cold water on everybody's joy today. Or I can go to the party and dance for the next five or ten years or however long God gives me.

I've made my decision. I'm going to the party! I'm going to take some dancing lessons. And I mean that literally. I just might sign up with Arthur Murray and learn how it's done. I'm not going to fake it as I once did when I went to a dance or be a wall flower when everyone else is on the dance floor. I'm going to learn how to do the western two-step. I'm going to learn how to do the chicken dance, the Macarena, the cupid shuffle, and whatever else they do at weddings.

How about you? Will you be stuck in the past with its fading joys and festering grievances and heartbreaking sorrows? Or will you let go and dance into a hopeful present full of the joys God is giving his children now and his promises for tomorrow?

For me, it's not a hard choice at all. I'm going to the dance. I'd like you to go there too. Even if you've been stuck in the past, glued to your chair, you don't need to stay there. You can get back on the dance floor, because it's never too late to dance.

Dance Steps — Questions For Reflection

1. What events in your past do you have a hard time moving beyond? How does hanging on to them benefit you? Or does it?
2. How does being stuck in the past interfere with your dancing in the present?
3. Is there anyone you don't want at your funeral? What in your heart would have to change for you to want them present?
4. How helpful is it for you to hear, or say, "You really need to get over it"? Why?
5. What flaws are you willing to acknowledge in a deceased loved one now that you were once unwilling to recognize? Why has this changed?
6. If you are divorced, name one or two things that were actually good about your marriage. Why is it hard to admit that the marriage wasn't all bad?
7. If you have changed churches, what was good about your former church? What did you dislike? Ask yourself the same questions about your present church.
8. How does Christ's loving and forgiving you affect your ability to love and forgive someone else?
9. Whom do you have the greatest trouble forgiving? Why?
10. What different circumstance in your family do you have trouble accepting? How will your thinking have to change if you are to feel more like dancing with your family *as it actually is*?
11. What specific steps will you take today to ensure that you will be dancing with your family tomorrow?

The Tenth Dance Step To Joy — Dance With Your Faith!

"For I am sure that neither death nor life, nor angels nor rulers, nor things present nor things to come, nor powers, nor height nor depth, nor anything else in all creation, will be able to separate us from the love of God in Christ Jesus our Lord."
Romans 8:38-39

Cultural confidence; that's a new term I heard on talk radio the other day. As coined by Anna Katrina Davey, cultural confidence is what enables companies to navigate successfully in a world of cultural differences.[21]

I don't recall the radio speaker's name, but right or wrong, he was borrowing the term and applying it to the current cultural confusion of our country. Cultural confidence, he contended, is what's needed for America to be at peace within itself and with the world. For him, cultural confidence was the certainty that our nation was founded on good and enduring values that we need not be ashamed of.

Yes, we've made some mistakes, he admitted — slavery, the mistreatment of Native Americans, persisting vestiges of racism, the excesses of capitalism — but that doesn't mean our system is all bad. On the contrary, the very constitution that created our nation and our democratic way of life is what has been correcting these problems.

No one else in the world has such a system, he said. People flock here from other countries to experience what we take for granted but what many of us now seem uncertain of. The *lack* of cultural confidence — that, according to the radio speaker — was the reason for many of our present problems. If we could only get our cultural confidence back, maybe our nation would be dancing again.

21 Anna Katrina Davey, "Cultural Confidence as a Paradigm for Peace" (Austin: www. interculturaltraining.com, 2007).

106

We could say the same thing about our Christian faith. My contention is that the church needs to regain its *spiritual* confidence. The reason there are about two billion Christians in the world today is because the church has offered a better way.[22]

It offers a way to God, centered on a loving Heavenly Father who gave his Son Jesus Christ to die on the cross so sinners could be saved, so we could be reconciled to God and to each other. Then, reconciled and forgiven, Christian faith offers us a way to live in peace *with* and respect *for* fellow believers, as well as with our neighbors who disagree with us. Believing in these truths is what I call spiritual confidence, certainty that our faith is good and redemptive and worth sharing with the world.

And yes, just like our nation, Christianity has had some bad moments. We've not always treated other cultures with respect. There have been Christian slave owners. We've done our share of massacring non-Christians, and sometimes even other Christians. In the Middle Ages, Catholics slaughtered the Orthodox in Constantinople. In my lifetime, Protestants and Catholics murdered each other in Ireland. And all of us have done our share of breaking God's commandments.

But just because *we've* messed up doesn't mean the whole Christian faith is bad. On the contrary, it's essentially good and wholesome. It's good and wholesome not just because of its doctrine, its teachings, but also because it moves us to aspire to *be* better and *do* better as human beings. Assured that God loves us and forgives us even when we sin, we try even harder to live our lives according to his hopes for us.

We do so joyfully because we are thankful for Jesus who died for us, and because the Holy Spirit dwells within us, giving us power and boldness to produce good fruit. As long as we are firmly convinced of this, we have *spiritual confidence*. And with spiritual confidence, we can dance with our faith and rejoice in being Christians.

It's popular these days to ridicule Christianity and accuse Christians of causing most — if not all — of the world's problems. Pastors and priests are portrayed as drunkards and

22 Conrad Hackett and David McClendon, "Christians remain world's largest religious group, but they are declining in Europe," Fact Tank, (Washington, D.C.: Pew Research Center, 2015).

sexual predators in movies. In old Westerns the preacher or missionary is usually a judgmental fool or an idealistic idiot. In casual conversation Christians are accused of being self-righteous hypocrites. Women are oppressed and minorities are mistreated because of Christians, we're told. Christians would abandon the poor, the sick and the elderly to a miserable death if they had their way. Christians are responsible for global warming and mass extinctions of animals and the disappearance of the rain forest.

These are the sorts of things we're constantly charged with. As the attacks have intensified, many Christians have become scared rabbits running for the nearest hole. We constantly hear the indictments against us but often say nothing in our own defense. As my former dentist once described himself, "I'm an agent in the Lord's secret service." In other words, he let no one know he was a Christian.

Many of the charges against Christianity and the Christian church are over-the-top nonsense. Every religious community of any kind has its share of rotten eggs. But the vast majority of pastors and priests are good and caring people, who constantly give of themselves to help others. It's Christians who are eager to forgive and help the morally fallen rebuild their lives. Hospitals, orphanages, public schools, colleges, social welfare programs, abolition of slavery and child labor, housing projects for the poor; all of these are past and ongoing efforts by Christians who have taken and still take their faith seriously. Caring for and restoring the environment comes right out of God's command to Adam and Eve to tend the garden. Today's Christian farmers, ranchers, miners, loggers, factory owners, and commercial fishermen have no interest in destroying the very gifts from God that allow them to make a living.

The next time you hear someone criticize or mock Christians, you might just point these things out to him. If you're actively involved in some caring outreach program in your community — and I hope you are — let the critics hear about what you do! And if you really want to have a positive influence in their lives, invite them to join you in volunteering. That way, rather than looking for a place to hide or hanging your head in shame, you can hold it high, dancing with confidence in your faith before the world.

Spiritual confidence isn't something that's based on science or reason. It's a gift from God. As the writer of Hebrews said, "Faith is the assurance of things hoped for, *the conviction of things not seen*" (Hebrews 11:1). You can't put the object of one's faith in a test tube. You can't examine it under a microscope. You can't send a rocket to a distant planet or star, get a piece of it and bring it home. It's something intangible but very real when you have it.

Faith means to trust in something, to rely on it, to adhere to it. It's staking your life on something you can't see or prove. But when you have it, it gives you a settled feeling of peace in whatever circumstances you find yourself. It allows you to dance hopefully and confidently even when things look bad and maybe get worse.

There are two kinds of faith that give us spiritual confidence as Christians, that move us to dancing. One kind of faith is Faith with a capital "F." It is "*The* Faith," *The* Faith that we read and confess in the creeds. It's *The* Faith taught by the church, our confession of the Holy Trinity, that God is One yet also three persons, Father, Son, and Holy Spirit. It's our confession that Jesus is the Son of God, *our* Savior and the Savior of the *whole world*.

If someone wants to know what you believe, share the creeds of the church with him. That's where the meat and potatoes — the solid stuff of The Faith — is spelled out for all the world to see. It's in the creeds that you find The Faith with a capital "F," The Faith we dance with.

Dr. Robert Preus, one of my seminary professors, said Martin Luther used to speak of "coal miner's faith," *fides carbonaria* in Latin. In Luther's day a coal miner was generally someone who had received very little in the way of education. So, a coal miner's faith was uninformed, untaught faith. It's what you have when you have no knowledge of what your church teaches. It went like this:

A man asked a coal miner, "What is it that you believe?"

The coal miner answered, "I believe whatever my church believes."

The man then asked him, "What is it that your church believes?"

The coal miner replied, "I don't know, but whatever it is, I believe it."

Coal miner's faith isn't something that gives us spiritual confidence. The Christian faith as summarized in the creeds is what gives us spiritual confidence. We firmly trust in, rely on and adhere to what we confess in the creeds. The creeds are what we confess at our baptism, our confirmation, in church on Sunday, before we receive Holy Communion, and hopefully in the hour of our death and at our funeral.

It is the content of the creeds that assure us that God our loving Father has forgiven us all our sins, and assured of an eternal home with him forever, all for the sake of his Son Jesus Christ who died for us, rose from the dead and is coming again. Cling to this Faith and you'll have spiritual confidence and a firm floor for dancing.

But spiritual confidence is more than trusting only in The Faith with a capital "F." It's also faith that is ours as a result of personal experience. That's what I call faith with a small "f." It's "*my* faith." *My* faith is my personal awareness and experience of God's presence in my life. It's a very subjective kind of thing.

There's an old gospel song that speaks of this kind of faith with a small "f." Here's one verse of the song along with the refrain:

I serve a risen Savior. He's in the world today.
I know that He is living, whatever men may say.
I see His hand of mercy, I hear His voice of cheer,
And just the time I need Him He's always near!

He lives, He lives, Christ Jesus lives today!
He walks with me and talks with me
Along life's narrow way!

110

The Tenth Dance Step

He lives, He lives, salvation to impart!
You ask me how I know He lives?
He lives within my heart.[23]

— Alfred Ackley — in the public domain

Now how do you explain that to someone, that Christ Jesus lives within your heart? How do you convince someone that Jesus is in the world today, that his hand of mercy is everywhere, that his voice cheers you, that he's near just when you need him most? How can you make someone believe that and experience the same thing you do? You can't!

You can't because that's your personal faith, faith with a small "f." It's God's gift to you. All you can do is pray that God will give someone else that gift of a very personal, sustaining faith, faith that will give them spiritual confidence, faith that will leave their heart dancing.

I think it's this kind of faith, faith with a small "f," that we want for our loved ones. Christian moms and dads rear their children in Christian homes. We read them Bible stories. We pray with them at bedtime. We say grace with them at meals. We bless them when they walk out the door. We take them to church where they're baptized, hear God's word, and get confirmed.

But despite our greatest and lifelong efforts, sometimes our children don't seem to evidence personal faith, faith with a small "f." They may not have denied The Faith with a capital "F," but neither have they evidenced personal faith with a small "f." And oh, how that worries us! How we yearn for them to know God personally and intimately as we do!

But you and I can't make that happen. All we can do is pray for them, love them, and live our faith before them. As we do, our confident hope is that eventually our baptized and taught children will someday experience the personal faith we parents so dearly want them to have, faith with a small "f."

I say this not out of mere optimism, but because God's word, the Bible, is full of promises to believing parents, promises such as these:

23 A. H. Ackley, song, "He Lives," in Inspiring Hymns (Grand Rapids: Singspiration Music, Division of Zondervan Corporation, 1974) # 124.

"Train up a child in the way he should go: and when he is old, he will not depart from it." (Proverbs 22:6)

And this: "I will establish my covenant between me and you and your offspring after you throughout their generations for an everlasting covenant, to be God to you and to your offspring after you... and I will be their God." (Genesis 17:7, 8b)

And this: "Repent and be baptized every one of you in the name of Jesus Christ for the forgiveness of your sins, and you will receive the gift of the Holy Spirit. For the promise is for you and for your children..." (Acts 2:38b-38a)

And this: "Let the little children come to me and do not hinder them, for to such belongs the kingdom of heaven." (Matthew 19:14b)

Do I need to go on? I don't think so. Spiritual confidence regarding our children is ours because of God's Word. We trust what is written there. We believe it in our hearts. And so even when our children don't always evidence the personal faith with a small "f" we'd like them to have, we dance joyfully anyway, leaving them in God's caring hands, trusting that in his time, he will give them that faith.

Spiritual confidence, dancing with our faith, is what keeps us from falling apart in the midst of the trials of life or in the face of death. It isn't something we can be taught. It's not a matter of spiritual discipline. It's a matter of personal experience of God's faithfulness over many years.

If I were to put pencil to paper, I could list event after event in which I have experienced the sustaining hand of God. I may not have felt his sustaining hand at the time. In fact, I may have believed that God had abandoned me to wallow in helplessness and despair. But the mere fact that today I am encouraging you to dance confidently with your faith is evidence that God didn't abandon me. On the contrary, he has been my "refuge and strength, a very present help in trouble" (Psalm 46:1). I suspect you have had those difficult experiences too.

In traditional marriage vows we promise to be faithful to our spouse, "for better, for worse, for richer, for poorer, in sickness and in health, until death parts us." As imperfect people, we haven't always kept our vows, but all of us have experienced the problems mentioned in those vows. We've experienced the worst life can throw at us — poverty, sickness, the death of loved ones.

But you and I still confess our faith. We still have spiritual confidence in our loving God. We firmly believe it is he who brought us through every trial we've ever endured. And because we're convinced of this, we're absolutely confident that he will bring us through whatever trials lie ahead. Those who have this kind of spiritual confidence find themselves rejoicing in their faith. They find themselves dancing with it.

It's what I call "having a track record with God." It's one of the nice things about getting old. When you're young and something catastrophic happens, you're terrified. You panic. You think it's the end of the world. You lose your girlfriend, your spouse, your job. Maybe you're in a bad accident. Maybe you have a health crisis or someone you love does. Like Chicken Little you think, "The sky is falling!" It isn't, but you feel that way.

As a matter of fact, most of what we think is a catastrophe isn't a catastrophe at all; it's really just an inconvenience. The days and weeks and months pass and the situation changes. Things improve. We have hope again. Looking back, we realize God brought us through it. As the Andrae Crouch song says, through everything we learn to trust in Jesus and depend upon his word.

Over and over something bad happens and over and over God brings us through it. So often do we go through these trials that finally when we're old and something bad happens, we don't panic and despair nearly as we did when we were young. God brought us through this kind of thing before. We know he'll do it again. We have a track record with God.

And even as we face death, we're confident that the Lord will travel with us through the valley, and soon we'll see Jesus who's never left us. It's on our death bed that Faith with a capital

"F" and faith with a small "f" come together, giving us spiritual confidence, giving us courage to dance as we embark on our journey through the darkness into the light on the other side.

Faith is the dance partner God gives us through all of life. Grab your partner! Hold her tight! As you do, you'll have confidence and joy whatever happens. And it can be your experience starting today, because it's never too late to dance!

Dance Steps — Questions For Reflection

1. How closely does "I'm an agent in the Lord's secret service" describe you? What description works better for you?
2. What in the history of the Christian church are you most ashamed of? What are you most proud of?
3. What community care or Christian outreach work are you involved in? How does this contribute to your spiritual confidence and dancing with your faith?
4. If you aren't currently volunteering, what outreach efforts might you be interested in learning more about? What would help you get involved, that is, get up and dance?
5. How is your personal faith with a small "f," *my* faith, different from or the same as your understanding of *The* Faith with a capital "F"?
6. If someone asks you, "What do you believe?" what will you say?
7. How confident are you in your faith: not very, somewhat, or very? What would make you feel more like dancing with spiritual confidence?
8. If you have learned by heart one or more of the three great creeds of the church, how does it affect your sense of spiritual confidence?
9. Is questioning your faith an indication of doubt or not? Is doubt the same as unbelief? Explain.
10. If you have children, what is your chief concern for them? How confident are you of their faith with a small "f"?
11. What is the toughest time you've gone through in life? How did God make his presence and love known?

The Eleventh Dance Step To Joy — Dance With Life In The Shadow Of Death!

"Even though I walk through the valley of the shadow of death, I will fear no evil, for you are with me; your rod and your staff, they comfort me. You prepare a table before me in the presence of my enemies…" Psalm 23:4-5

Once a month for many years I conducted a chapel service at a retirement home in Rio Rancho. On the way to an open space living room area where we held the service, I'd often stop and greet the residents, like Mabel.

Mabel stood out from all the rest. She was a hundred years old. Every time I saw her, she looked like she was going to a party. She'd be wearing a dress and her hair would be beauty parlor perfect. She always had her makeup on — rouge, bright red lipstick, even eye shadow. On her left shoulder, a flower corsage would be pinned. Her walker would be decorated by her daughter for the seasons. Every time I saw Mabel she would ask me about my family. She knew I was married and had three sons and wanted to know how everyone was doing. Whatever I shared with her, she seemed to remember.

As much as everyone loved Mabel, and as full of life as she was, Mabel was a realist. She knew she wouldn't be around much longer. Down the hall on the door to her apartment was a sign that read, "DNR — DNI." Those letters stand for, "Do Not Resuscitate. Do Not Intubate." That meant should Mabel stop breathing, she didn't want any special measures taken to bring her back. She wanted to be left alone to die when nature took its course. But until then, Mabel was dancing with life, loving every moment of it. How could she do that, knowing that at her age she was practically at death's door? How can you and I do that, how can we dance with life in the shadow of death?

One thing that can help us dance as we face life's end is to have a death plan. Earlier I talked about the importance of having a life plan. Well, a death plan can be just as important. A well thought out death plan combined with the resources of faith can relieve us of a great deal of stress and worry during our last days in this world. Once we have our death plan in place, we can look at it from time to time just to make sure we've done everything we can to prepare for our passing. Then we can get on with the dance of life, worry free, having exercised some responsibility and control over what's important to us while our mind is still intact.

I know this may sound morbid and a bit creepy, but we really need to face the fact that no one leaves this planet alive. Well, maybe that's changing. As I write this, a mission to Mars is being discussed that will require the astronauts to live and die somewhere else. No provision is being made to bring them back to earth. But whether we happen to be on Mars or any other place in the galaxy, we don't get out alive. We have to die some place.

Since that's our personal reality, we can either let someone else plan our death or we can plan it ourselves. By planning our death, I don't mean deciding when and how we are going to die. That's God's business, his secret. We're not party to that information. What I'm referring to are such things as completing and filing a medical directives form, planning for the distribution of our property, determining what kind of funeral or memorial service we will have or not have, and what legacy we want to leave behind for those we care about.

Fortunately, we live in a country with laws that require our next of kin or guardians to respect our wishes when those wishes are written down in legal documents and then signed, notarized, and kept on file. Our authority lives on in these important pieces of paper even after we're gone.

King Solomon bemoaned the fact that he ultimately had no control over what would happen to his property when he died. Said Solomon,

"I must leave it to the man who will come after me, and who knows whether he will be wise or a fool? Yet he will be master of all for which I toiled and used my wisdom under the sun. This also is vanity."
(Ecclesiastes 2:18b-19)

The king's fears were realized when his foolish son, Rehoboam, inherited Solomon's kingdom and wealth and then promptly lost half of everything.

It doesn't have to be that way for you and me if we have a death plan expressing exactly what we want to happen to us and our property at life's end. If we don't have a plan, someone's going to make a plan for us and we may or may not feel like dancing with what they come up with. Suppose, for example, you have a medical incident. It is so severe that life support is required to keep you breathing and your heart beating. Also, let's suppose there's no real likelihood of your getting better or having any quality of life, ever again.

If you've not completed a legally binding medical directive instructing first responders or the hospital medical staff as to what care or treatment you want, you're probably going to be kept alive in a vegetative state, possibly for a very long time. Or if family members are present, they will make that decision, or they will argue among themselves and be indecisive forcing the medical staff to make a de facto decision or ask a judge to make one.

As a pastor, I witnessed an elderly patient receive CPR three times when family members refused to let him die peacefully. Most of the bones in his rib cage were broken by the time the medical team had to quit. It was not my place to tell the family what to do. I was there to provide emotional and spiritual support. The patient could have spared his relatives considerable emotional trauma by letting them know in advance his desires.

On another occasion, I sat with a family after their elderly relative endured a massive heart attack in the Cardiac Intensive Care Unit. The doctor came into the family consultation room saying, "There's a very small chance I could save him with surgery. Even if he survives, he will never be the same. What would you like me to do?" The family debated for a few moments and then opted for the surgery. The patient died on the operating table. Again, all that emotional agony — not to mention the huge financial burden incurred — could have been avoided had the patient completed a form expressing his wishes in a medical directive.

Nobody is dancing in such situations. Specially trained social workers, nurses and sometimes hospital chaplains can help you put down in writing what levels of care you want. Once you get it done, post it on your bedroom door and provide copies to your family, your doctor and your hospital, and then you can breathe a sigh of relief. You can begin to feel good about what you've done and get on with the business of life, dancing.

Another part of a good death plan is an up-to-date will. I'm amazed at the number of otherwise responsible adults who have no will. All of us have possessions of some kind that need to be distributed when we die. Even if we are very poor and think we own nothing, usually we own something, even if it's only of sentimental value. But probably most of us have something more; a bank account, or investments, or insurance, or a pension, or maybe we own a house or land or vehicles. Who will get our property?

If you don't have a Last Will and Testament, the state decides who gets your property and how it will be divided up. In my state, New Mexico, if the deceased is married, the surviving spouse gets the property. But maybe you don't live in a community property state. Check with your lawyer to find out.

If you don't have a will, it's likely the court will decide how to divide your property up after your debts are paid. Probably the judge will allot your assets equally among your next of kin, maybe your children. But what if one of your children is severely handicapped and requires more resources for personal care than his siblings? Do you really want them all to have an equal share? Or what if one of your children is a spendthrift, a drug addict, or a gambler and he's already depleted your assets, do you want to reward that kind of behavior?

You can decide who gets what with a will. You may even decide your family is sufficiently well off and really doesn't need anything at all of what you've got. Maybe there are certain charities, churches, or non-profits that you would like to receive a portion of, or even your entire estate. You could still leave a token amount to family members as an expression of your love.

I've never forgotten what a planned giving counselor, Reverend Richard Holz, once shared at a will awareness seminar he gave for church people. "How long do think the average inheritance lasts after it is distributed to the heirs?" he asked. No one in the room had any idea. Here's his answer, "Eighteen days."

Eighteen days! Can you imagine that? This was twenty years ago so maybe the statistic has changed. But I doubt it. You work, save, and invest for a lifetime to accumulate a nest egg so you might have something to provide for your needs in old age or leave to your heirs and they spend it in eighteen days!

This sounds like echoes of Solomon's fears realized to me. If your heirs are likely to be irresponsible with your estate, you might want to start thinking about whether to leave a significant portion of it to the charity of your choice where it can do some eternal good. Doing so can give you some peace of mind and leave your heart dancing.

What about all those personal items of sentimental value that may not be itemized for distribution through a will? I've often visited with elderly people who tell me things like, "That quilt was my grandmother's. I want it to go to my granddaughter." Chances are the granddaughter will never see it unless it is marked as being for her. Better yet, Grandma can make a point of giving it to her granddaughter in person to make sure she gets it.

Here's why I suggest that. The mother of a family friend died far away from New Mexico in North Carolina. Our friend managed to make it to the funeral, but because of her teaching job she couldn't be there to clean out the house. There were special items her mother had said she could have but when she finally got home again to help, all those special items had either been claimed by her brothers and sisters or sold. My friend was very hurt and her relationship with her family ended in bitterness.

That would never have happened if the mother had given the promised items to her daughter before she died or if she had marked them as being for the daughter and told the other siblings her wishes. Had she done that, everyone might have been dancing and the family relationship might have continued. A good death plan would have helped.

At death, many of us are likely to leave behind a houseful of stuff, some of it valuable, much of it junk. If we're not particularly neat and organized, the average house and garage can be packed with fifty or sixty years of stuff that needs to be gone through and disposed of. Do you really want your heirs going through all this accumulation, some of it very private, some of it maybe even embarrassing? I remember seeing some of my Dad's World War II Navy pictures from Honolulu. There are reasons they were locked away in a trunk.

You can minimize the daunting task loved ones will face, and also maintain your dignity even after you die, if your death plan includes organizing and disposing of all this stuff yourself. If you're frail, sick or elderly, get someone to help you. Pay someone if necessary. Let the helper keep whatever they want. But just get it done!

My sister Suzanne has a great system for dealing with lifetime collections of junk. Everything you own can be divided up, generally speaking anyway, into three piles. Pile 1 is "What I need." The "What I Need" pile includes essential clothing, furniture, kitchen utensils, office supplies, medicines, and the like. It's everything I absolutely must have to survive. Keep everything in the "What I Need" pile.

Pile 2 is "What I Love." This is where I put things I don't actually need to survive but I'm so attached to, I can't let them go. I have a few books like that. Most of my books I've already gotten rid of since they just collected dust and I never looked at them. But a few of them I really love and never get tired of. Even if I seldom look at them, I can't bear the thought of giving them up. These I keep.

Pile 3 is the "What I Don't Need and Don't Love" pile. If your house is like mine, much of your stuff is in this category. If you don't love it and don't need it, chances are no one else in your family wants it either. I have boxes of old hardware, partially used landscaping supplies, worn out tools, old costumes, bits and pieces of this and that, old class notes, sermons no one will ever read, clothes I haven't worn for years and on and on. I hang on to this stuff, thinking I might need it. So far I've gone through three moves to different houses and some of this stuff has never been unpacked. As a rule of thumb, if you haven't looked at it for three years, you don't need it. Get rid of it.

As you get the three piles rhythm of organizing and disposing of things going, you'll probably find it's quite exhilarating taking carload after carload of stuff to Goodwill or to the landfill. If you're into garage sales, you can get rid of a lot of it that way too and turn some trash into cash in the process. I can almost guarantee that the more stuff you get rid of, the more relieved you'll feel. In fact, you'll feel like dancing.

But a good death plan involves more than just medical directives and property distribution. I strongly recommend a Christian Will to be included as a preamble to your Last Will and Testament. I credit Reverend Holz with giving me this idea as well. A Christian Will is written testimony to your faith, your values, and your hopes for your family.

When people show up for the reading of the will, usually the distribution of the property is the only thing on their minds. This is your opportunity to get them to think about something else, if only briefly. For a few minutes they will hear your voice giving witness through the written word to your faith, values, and hopes for your family. This is your chance to be like Joseph, revealing your faith, dreams, and prophesies for the people you love.

This is the one and only time they will all be there, listening to what was most important to you in life. For Christians that would be the good news of Jesus Christ and his love as evidenced by his suffering and death on the cross for sinners. Christians are often troubled that they have never been able to give a clear witness to their loved ones of their faith in Christ and how he has blessed them. A Christian Will provides that opportunity. Once you've written it down, you can dance knowing your loved ones will hear.

There's one thing left to be arranged in a good death plan, and that's how you want your passing to be acknowledged, or your life and faith celebrated. At the beginning of my ministry in the 1970s, almost everyone who died, Christian or not, had a funeral. It took place in a church or at a mortuary with the body present in a casket, either open or closed. Most people just assumed that's how it would be done, so it was.

As our culture has grown increasingly unchurched and secular, far fewer people think this is important. Nowadays it's very common for older believing adults who are church members to have grown children who do not share their faith and are not members of any religious group. Thus, in the last fifteen years or so, I would say that half or more of my church members who died did not have funerals or memorial services. Why? Because their children did not want one. Not only that, very few of my church members were buried. Most were cremated because it was cheaper.

I strongly suggest that if you believe it is important to acknowledge your value to God and the role of faith in your life, you write down your wishes regarding a funeral or memorial service. Share this with your pastor so that it can be filed in the church office. Also, see to it that the members of your family responsible for your final affairs get copies. It will be far more difficult for them to ignore your desires if you've done this.

And if you are financially able, prearrange your funeral or memorial service with the mortuary of your choosing. If it's prepaid, it's going to happen. It'll happen even if you move and die somewhere else. The mortuary where you made the arrangements will work with the mortuary in your last place of residence. Doing this will ease your mind and make you feel more like dancing.

What about burial or cremation? Which one should you choose? In the early days of Christianity, many non-Christians were cremated. It was widely believed in the world of the ancient Greeks and Romans that the soul was eternal but not the body. Therefore, cremation made sense to them. But Christians have always maintained as an article of faith that upon the return of Christ, the body will be raised to new life and reunited with the soul to live forever in a new and restored world. For Christians, burial of the body was an affirmation of this belief in resurrection and cremation was a denial of it.

But whether one is buried in the ground or buried at sea, the body eventually deteriorates and disappears. Even so, according to Christian belief, on the last day, the body will be raised to life. This being an article of faith, many Christian churches in recent years have concluded that cremation is no longer a denial of the resurrection of the body and so they have allowed it.

Whichever one you choose, your children or other next of kin need to know. Put it in your death plan to let them know what you prefer. If they are not Christians and you don't specify, they will likely have your body cremated, even if that's not what you want. So, tell them your desire, check it off your list and get on with the dance.

So far we've talked about the earthly or worldly aspect of a death plan. But what about the spiritual aspects? Maybe you've done everything your death plan calls for to insure an orderly conclusion to your earthly affairs. And you are at peace about that. You are dancing over having completed everything on your list. But what about actually dying? What about the moment of death? How can you have peace in your heart and actually let go and leave this world peacefully when the time comes?

I've found that Psalm 23 helps me as I contemplate that moment. Psalm 23 is probably the most beloved passage in the Bible. Almost everyone asks for it during funeral planning, either for their own or someone else's service. It's easy to see why. Think of these words, "Even though I walk through the valley of the shadow of death, I will fear no evil, for you are with me" (v. 4).

Why are these words so comforting? They tell us that none of us dies alone. Our Good Shepherd, the Lord, is with us on our journey. A shepherd won't leave his sheep in a crevasse or a hole or tangled in the briars. Our shepherd pulls his sheep to safety, he untangles them from the snares, he carries them across the dangerous rocks, he makes sure they get to green pastures with abundant water. It's comforting to think of ourselves as those sheep.

There's something else I like about this psalm. It speaks of "the valley of the shadow of death." If there's a shadow, what does that imply there must also be? What do you need in order to make a shadow? Yes, sunlight! Our Good Shepherd leads and carries us through the valley of the shadow of death to sunlight and life on the other side. What a comforting and reassuring picture that is! I can dance with that picture, can't you?

Now meditate for a moment on these words, "You prepare a table before me in the presence of my enemies." The image is of the psalmist, David, eating his lunch on a battlefield, with the enemy looking on. How could David happily eat his meal without a care in the world while an armed enemy is poised to do him harm? The Lord was his shepherd, that's how. The Good Shepherd was not going to allow the enemy to hurt his sheep. David knew that. The enemy knew that. So, David peacefully ate his lunch, worry free.

I see this psalm as a metaphor for the Lord's Supper, Holy Communion. I see it as a metaphor for Holy Baptism. I see it as a metaphor for anointing of the sick. Our spiritual enemies are guilt, death and fear of the unknown. But as Christians, we believe our sins are nailed to the cross with Jesus and our guilt washed away in the still waters of Baptism. In Holy Communion we feast on God's forgiveness at the table he sets for us. When we're sick and anointed, we're reminded of our baptism and reassured of God's promise of resurrection. These holy rites reaffirm God's promise that none of our enemies has any power over us at all. They just stand at a distance and watch helplessly. I can dance with that, can't you?

I can also dance with the Bible's images of the beautiful world God has in store for us, a world that contrasts markedly with this often painful present one. It goes by several names, heaven, paradise, Zion, the promised land. However you choose to name it, it's a place where death is swallowed up forever, where God wipes away our tears, and where all our shame is taken away (Isaiah 25:6-8). It's a place where infants don't die and people don't get forced out of their houses or where farmers don't plant crops for an enemy to steal. Everyone who lives there gets to enjoy the work of their hands. It's a place of peace between nations and harmony with nature (Isaiah 65:17-25). I can dance with that picture, can't you?

The New Testament promises even more. In describing his ministry to John the Baptist, Jesus said, "the blind receive their sight and the lame walk, lepers are cleansed and the deaf hear, and the dead are raised up, and the poor have good news preached to them" (Matthew 11:5). Few experienced such blessings then or even now, but all of us enjoy them in the wonderful world that's coming.

In the Book of Revelation, John the Apostle describes heaven as a great walled city, with the water of life flowing through it, with the tree of life offering abundant fruit to everyone, its gates always left open because there's no more danger. There are no lamps there because Jesus himself is its light (Revelation 21:9-26).

There are common themes in all these pictures of the new life we look forward to after we walk through the valley of the shadow of death; no more suffering or tears or death. There's no more war. There's no danger of any kind. No one is sick or lame or blind or in prison. There's useful work for us all to do. God himself is with us there. Why are we given all these beautiful images? So we can live today joyfully and face death tomorrow confidently as we dance on our journey to forever.

I remember a folk song popular years ago. It was written and sung by Woodie Guthrie in 1963. The first verse speaks of walking a lonesome valley and doing it all by yourself. You can find the lyrics on the internet.

I love the song but I don't see it that way. Jesus walked the lonesome valley for us. He died for us and rose again to take the fear and sting out of walking that valley when it's time for us to go. Not only did Jesus walk it in our place, he joins us on our journey and walks with us every step of the way. We don't "gotta walk it" by ourselves. In fact, we can look at that valley and even dance as the time draws near. And it's never too late to dance.

Dance Steps — Questions For Reflection

1. How hard is it for you to talk about and make a death plan? Why is it difficult to confront one's own death? Or is it?
2. Do you have a medical directive form completed, signed and filed with your doctor, hospital, and family? Is it readily accessible in your home? Why or why not?
3. Who or what charitable organizations will get your property when you die? How can you be sure?
4. When you die, if you still have minor children, who will be legally responsible for their care, physically and spiritually? Note: legal guardians and godparents or sponsors in baptism are not necessarily the same unless you have spelled that out in your will. Have you done this?
5. Why is it important that you have a will even if you don't have much property?
6. What special items do you want to go to certain people? How will you be sure they get them?
7. Why might it be good to dispose of some personal items before you die?
8. What are your most treasured beliefs and values? If you have a will, have you included these beliefs and values in the preamble?
9. What sort of service do you want when you die, if any? Do you want to be buried or cremated? How will you know your wishes will be carried out?
10. Read: Psalm 23; Isaiah 25:6-9; Isaiah 65:17-25; John 3:16; John 14:1-6; Romans 6:3-5; Romans 8:35-39; Thessalonians 4:13-18; and Revelation 21:1-5. Which of these do you find most comforting? Which leaves you dancing with spiritual confidence? If you have a funeral, memorial, or celebration of life service, which of these, or others, do you want read?
11. How might having a completed death plan and check list actually help you dance?

The End Of The Matter (Or Maybe The Beginning?)

"The end of the matter; all has been heard. Fear God and keep his commandments, for this is the whole duty of man."
Ecclesiastes 12:13

One of the most interesting characters in the "Marco Polo" TV series is One Hundred Eyes. He's the blind martial arts instructor assigned to teach Marco Polo how to fight. One Hundred Eyes combines sword fighting with frequent wise sayings. Here's one I seized on: "A man wishing to be unhappy finds many ways to prove his course.[24]

What's that mean? It means that if you and I are determined to be unhappy, we'll always find reasons to be that way. I've met people determined to be unhappy, haven't you? It doesn't matter if the sun is shining and the day is beautiful, they'll find something to complain about. On the other hand, if someone is determined to be happy, they'll find reasons to dance.

You and I always have reasons to dance, things to rejoice in. Even if it hasn't been your style and you've habitually been a down-in-the-dumps person, you can change. *Because it's never too late to dance.*

In the preceding chapters, I've laid out how you can make joyful dancing happen, no matter where you are in the timeline of life. It's a matter of choosing how you will think and behave, and refusing to be a passive victim.

One can live in a shack and joyfully serve God and one's neighbor. Just ask Maria, who found happiness cooking for mission teams even though she lived in shack. One can be locked away in a prison awaiting trial and eventual execution and still rejoice. Just ask Saint Paul who still managed to pray for people he loved and send them encouraging messages.

24 Marco Polo, created by John Fusco, featuring Tom Wu (Hundred Eyes), Netflix, 2014..

I haven't yet mentioned Pastor Meiners. He had a debilitating illness that landed him in a wheelchair. In order to preach, he would have to be lifted up, wheelchair and all, to the altar area of his church. I remember one day he addressed the congregation and said he could no longer preach or even come to church. But even so, he would be available at his home office to meet with anyone who needed pastoral care. He would listen and pray with them and do so till he died. And that's exactly what he did, joyfully. Pastor Meiners danced as long as he still had breath.

Dancing, my word for joy, is a choice. We don't have to wait for something good to happen to us. We can choose to look at things in positive ways and make decisions that are good for us and those we love. There is no reason to feel guilty about dancing. You are a child of God who loves you and who dances over you. He rejoiced when he created you and when he was finished, he called you good. When you wandered away, he rejoiced when you found your way back home and he held a party for you. So go ahead and dance, it's okay!

I've pointed out that you and I were made in the image of God and that metaphorically speaking God dances. We see that in the joy expressed in the psalms. We see it in the story of the prodigal son when the father in the parable gives a party with dancing because his wayward son has come home.

We see it in the story of Jesus going to the wedding feast where he performed his first miracle, turning water into wine. Wine, joy, and dancing all go together at wedding feasts. Scripture speaks of Israel as being the bride of God and the church being the bride of Christ. For Israel, the wedding dance was the Exodus. For Christians the wedding dance is the empty tomb of Jesus. The wedding feast is now in progress! The band is playing! Are your dancing shoes on?

If you aren't already dancing, you can get on the floor any time. I pray that these *Eleven Dance Steps To Joy* will help you get there. They are the fruit of what I've learned from my training as a pastor, counselor, and chaplain and what I've experienced personally. They are lessons I have learned from my mistakes as well as my successes. When I follow these *Eleven Dance Steps To*

Joy, I find myself to be a happy person, a person who dances with life. When I don't, I find myself a miserable wall flower. I don't like being a miserable wall flower and I don't think you do either. So, get off your chair, put on your dancing shoes, and get out on that floor!

In case you don't remember what the *Eleven Dance Steps To Joy* are, I'll review them briefly:

First, dance with a life plan. Many of us go through life as though we're the metal ball in an arcade pin ball machine being whacked around by the little levers until we fall in the hole. We are acted upon, but we don't willfully act on our own. We put in our seventy years, or eighty if there is strength, as the Bible says, and we die. Maybe our life has been a success. Maybe not. We don't know which it is because we never had a life plan to evaluate our success by.

It doesn't have to be that way. You can choose to write out your life plan today and then follow it! Start living according to what fits *you* best. Then, as the sunset of your life nears, you can dance and say, "I'm a complete success, because *I did it my way*." Many thanks to Frank Sinatra for that last thought.

Second, dance with who you are! In order to have a life plan that fits us, we need to take a thorough inventory of ourselves — our personality, our likes and dislikes, our strengths and weaknesses, our qualities and values. If we take all these factors into consideration, the life plan we create will more accurately reflect who we are and we'll be more likely to stick with it.

When I graduated from seminary the first time, I didn't have a call. With a wife and small child, I had to find a job. This was back when affirmative action was really big. Frustration met me at every turn. I wasn't the right color. I wasn't bilingual. I was the wrong gender. I tried getting hired by an appliance store, and then a potash mine. Nobody would hire me. I really didn't like the idea of working in any of those places anyway so my heart wasn't exactly broken.

So with no call in hand I tried starting churches, two of them. But I'm no Billy Graham and neither one took off. Reluctantly I went back to seminary. It was the right decision. After additional study I received my first real call, then another, and another. I've been able to spend most of my working life doing exactly what I wanted. I didn't know what life plans were back then, but a personal life plan is what I had been following unconsciously all along.

As I evaluate myself, I fully realize I'm a pretty ordinary pastor. But according to my life plan and who I have discovered myself to be, I'm a smashing success! Can you imagine how miserable I would have been had I gotten a job in a potash mine running the mucker? Thankfully, the Holy Spirit was guiding me into what was right *for me*. He helped me figure out who I was and dance with it. He'll do the same for you. Find out who you are and then get on the dance floor!

Third, dance with those you love! God loves everybody and is intimately concerned with the details of every person's life. But you and I aren't God and we don't have an eternity to concern ourselves with the needs of everyone we encounter every day. When I spent every waking minute trying to help everyone in need in my church and community, I neglected my family and provoked them and myself to resentment. I had my priorities wrong.

St. Paul says, *"Anyone who does not provide for his own relatives and especially for those of his own household, has denied the faith and is worse than an unbeliever."* (1 Timothy 5:8) Ouch! If you discover that to be you, admit it to God, embrace his forgiveness, get your priorities in order and then dance with the fresh start God gives you. The sign on a church I drove by identified itself as the "Second Chance Church." I've needed lots of second chances. Haven't you? God is always happy to give them. Take all the second chances you need and get back in the dance.

"Husbands, love your wives as Christ loved the church and gave himself up for her," says Saint Paul (Ephesians 5:25). We refer to this often in premarital counseling. As Jesus gave himself up for the church, husbands are to be like Jesus, giving themselves up for their wives. But husbands are not Jesus. Jesus gave himself up for everyone. It's not the job of spouses to give themselves up for their neighbors, their business or even their church if they

happen to be pastors. Family comes first. The best of everything we have is for them. Keep that priority straight and there will be dancing in your home.

Fourth, dance free from that rope! Maybe I should phrase this differently. Maybe I should say, "Dance with the ropes *you* choose, not the ropes that *others* choose for you." I think many of the ropes we choose to grab are guilt ropes. We jump in and try to rescue people when they need help because we feel guilty if we don't, or because someone has badgered us into doing it. You can tell when you've unwillingly grabbed someone else's rope because you feel angry and resentful the whole time you're hanging on to it.

Jesus didn't grab ropes that people threw at him unless they fit his life plan. His life plan was focused on suffering and dying on the cross to redeem the lost. He didn't let himself get distracted. Once when someone demanded he get in the middle of an inheritance dispute and resolve it, he refused. He said, "Man, who made me a judge or arbitrator over you?" (Luke 12:14). Maybe the plaintiff had a legitimate case but Jesus didn't grab that rope. It would just get in the way of him fulfilling his life plan.

There are lots of worthy people who need help. There are lots of good organizations and charities that we could support and participate in. But we can't do everything. When the demand for help comes your way, stack it up against your life plan. It if fits, by all means grab the rope! If it doesn't, in a kind way and with a good conscience simply refuse the rope.

Irresponsible people are counting on you to feel guilty. They'll manipulate you with guilt if they can. Don't fall for it! Grab ropes that fit your life plan, that you decide to dance with. Remember you are a child of God with two hands, not five like a starfish, or eight legs like a spider. You can only do some much. Accept your limitations, throw back as many ropes as you have to, and dance with a happy conscience.

Fifth, dance as you discover God! I love kids because they're full of questions about God and they aren't afraid to ask them. They can also spot phony answers that don't make sense and they aren't afraid to say so. Adults figure out where the land mines of faith are and they don't go there. They've learned what questions not to ask, and they're satisfied with answers that might sound silly to a kid.

I'm trying to be a kid again as I rediscover God on the threshold of my old age. I'm on firm ground in doing so since Jesus says, "Truly I tell you, unless you change and become like little children, you will never enter the kingdom of heaven" (Matthew 18:3). I'm done with pat answers. I want to know the truth. And if the truth isn't for me to know, I don't want a phony pat answer in its place.

Recently over lunch, my friend Roger asked, "Why would it have been wrong for Jesus to be married?" My initial reaction was to start parroting answers. With difficulty, I restrained myself. Roger went on, "God made men and women and said they were good and if he ordained marriage, and if Jesus was like us in every way except sin, why would it have been wrong for Jesus to be married? It wouldn't have been sin, would it?"

This was a question I'd never thought of. Like Porky Pig, I just stammered at first, "Ba deep, ba deep, ba deep." Then I took a theological approach but quickly realized I didn't know what I was talking about. Finally I just said, "Roger, I really don't know. All I know is that there's nothing in the Bible that says Jesus was married. And if he had been, it would have been a huge distraction from his primary purpose to die on the cross to save sinners."

A friend, Walter, once shared a verse with me. It says, "The secret things belong to the Lord our God, but the things that are revealed belong to us and to our children forever, that we may do all the words of this law" (Deuteronomy 29:29). The idea is that some things are just none of our business. But other things are for us to know and teach our children. So these are the things we focus on. These are things we can dance with.

Sixth, dance with every success. A few years ago, as I was working on my Model T Ford coupe, the trunk lid fell on my left index finger, almost completely cutting it off. I wrapped my finger in a handkerchief and had a friend drive me to the hospital.

The ER staff tried to find an orthopedic surgeon to sew it back on. But they all refused even to try. They were afraid they couldn't do it right.

Finally, the ER doctor, Dr. Winchester, said he'd give it a try. He cleaned up my finger, put it back in place, and sewed it together as best he could. Then he told me, "You'll probably lose that finger. But even if you don't, you'll definitely lose the fingernail." Guess what? I didn't lose anything. I still have my finger and even the nail. Unfortunately, my finger ended up a little crooked. I suppose Dr. Winchester, if he knew about it, could beat himself up over leaving me with a crooked finger. But I'm not unhappy with it. The main thing is I still have my finger and, perfect or not, it works. That's worth celebrating. It's worth dancing over!

Unrealistic expectations can crush us. Fear of failure can keep us from trying anything. Nobody's perfect. And we don't have to be. Jesus has been perfect for us. Believing that sets us free from the impossible burden of perfectionism. It gives us permission both to fail without shame as well as celebrate the little successes in life.

Life is made up of thousands of little steps and actions. Any little step or action done well is worth celebrating, even if there's failure right beside it. Maybe your garden was a disaster but the zucchini did really well; dance with that! Maybe the book you wrote didn't get published but the editor really liked one chapter; dance with that! Maybe the paint on the street rod you built peeled off, but the engine ran perfectly; dance with that! Maybe you didn't get into Harvard, but you did get into New Mexico Highlands - dance with that! Look for the little successes, celebrate them, and dance with them.

Seventh, dance with contentment. I shared with my sister Suzanne the fable of the rope. That's the story about the man who finally knew what he wanted out of life and started on a journey to find it. But after he set out, he got stopped on a bridge by a stranger with a rope tied around his waist. The stranger tossed the traveler the end of the rope then jumped off the bridge, telling the traveler to hold on or the stranger would fall to this death.

The traveler had to decide what he was going to do, let go of the rope and continue on his journey, or stand there forever holding on, literally being roped into someone's problem he didn't want to be responsible for.

I asked my sister what she would do. She replied, "I wouldn't be on the bridge in the first place. I'm very content with my life the way it is." I hadn't expected that answer. It never occurred to me that there was another way to look at the fable. But she makes a good point. Happy people are content. They're thankful for their families, their homes, their communities, and their jobs as they already are. They're not sitting around being miserable wishing things were different, scheming and cooking up ways to exchange one set of circumstances for another.

Ambition isn't necessarily bad, but it is if the motive is ingratitude. People who dance rejoice in who they are and what they have now, even if they strive to improve their circumstances. Sometimes you can improve things, sometimes you can't. In prison, there wasn't much Saint Paul could do to make his circumstances better. But he was okay with that. He said, "I have learned in whatever situation I am to be content" (Philippians 4:11). When you've learned the secret of contentment — gratitude, a thankful heart — you can dance even in prison.

Eighth, Dance with Your Work! Some people look at their job as if it was some kind of slavery. They count the days until the weekend, until their vacation, or until they can retire. There's a radio show called "Money Talk" with Bob Brinker. I sometimes catch it on Sunday afternoons. The host talks about "critical mass." Critical mass to him is the point at which your debts are all paid off and you have enough cash flow so you don't have to work anymore.

But since when is work a bad thing? God designed us to work. The Bible tells us that God made Adam and Eve and put them in the Garden of Eden and told them to tend it. Tending a garden is work. Most people feel a need to work or at least do something useful. I know I'm that way. I've held a job since I was fifteen and can't stand being idle. Some people hate work and seem unhappy with their job no matter what it is. But work is good for us! God works. He made the universe and keeps it going. We were made in his image and that's why there's something in us that makes us want to work.

Before the COVID-19 pandemic, my wife Kathy and I walked at the Cottonwood Mall each morning whenever we could for exercise. At the mall there was a toy train you could ride. For a couple of bucks you could hop in and go from one end of the mall to the other and back. Everyone loved seeing the train. About the only people who didn't love it were the drivers. They seemed embarrassed and bored by what they were doing. They looked about as happy as someone in the doctor's office waiting for a colonoscopy.

But just before the holidays I saw a new driver. What a different attitude he had! He was wearing bib overalls, a blue shirt, a red bandana around his neck and an engineer's cap on his head. He was smiling and waving and ringing the bell. And guess what? There were far more kids and parents waiting to board! Why? Because he was dancing with his work. I rarely rode the train, but even I was tempted to buy a ticket. I felt like dancing right on board.

Saint Paul said, "Whatever you do, whether you eat or drink, do it all to the glory of God" (1 Corinthians 10:31). When you do whatever it is that you do to the glory of God, you'll find yourself dancing with your job.

Ninth, dance with your past into your future. Every year I get a few Christmas letters in the mail. They're mostly full of accomplishments and successes the family wants their friends and relatives to know about. They tell us about graduations, new jobs, promotions, vacations, reunions, and so on. They usually leave out the other stuff; things like getting arrested for drunk driving, your daughter becoming a Satan worshiper, and losing at the casino all the money you were going to spend on the family vacation.

But that bad stuff is what other people would really like to read about, right? It's also where we learn our most valuable lessons. From the bad stuff we learn about God's grace and forgiveness. We learn to forgive ourselves, to give ourselves and our family members a second chance and bring something beautiful out of the messes we get ourselves into.

In my Kansas congregation I met Fay, (not her real name). Fay was a woman whose past was colorful, to say the least. Her mother had helped start the church and Fay had a great upbringing. But as a young woman Fay took a different path than her mother. She became a bar fly and a homewrecker. After thoroughly messing up her life and the lives of several other people, Fay came back to church, she grew strong in her faith and she became the president of the women's group in the congregation. I never met a finer or more reliable church member than Fay.

Fay never denied any of what she'd done; she never tried to paper it over. In fact, she came to visit me and told me the whole story right after I got there since she knew I'd hear it from someone. Late in life Fay had come to her senses. Somewhat like the prodigal son she came home to her heavenly Father and built a new life for herself. Fay's faithfulness was a reason for me to dance. I did her funeral in Santa Fe many years ago. I have no doubt that Fay is now dancing in heaven with Jesus.

You don't need to hide your past. It's part of your identity. Embrace it boldly as having helped make you who you are today. With the assurance of God's forgiveness, you can dance with your past, right on into eternity.

Tenth, dance with your faith! In seminary, Dr. Robert Preus, my professor of Christian dogmatics, provided me with the helpful distinction between "The Faith" and "my faith." "The Faith" with a capital "F" is what the church has always confessed to be true. "The Faith" is what we boldly proclaim to the world. It is what the church says it believes as articulated in the three great ecumenical creeds. Most Christian churches regularly read aloud one or more of these creeds during worship services or as the sacraments are administered.

Members of congregations are expected to acknowledge these beliefs as their own. But "The Faith" one acknowledges is not necessarily the same thing one experiences emotionally or subjectively. One's personal experience of God is "my faith," faith with a small "f." It is the intimate sense of God's presence and the assurance of his saving and caring love. "My faith" for many Christians is what they would describe as their "relationship" with God. It is so meaningful and essential to them that they want their loved ones and friends to experience the same thing. This desire often becomes the chief concern of their prayer and devotional life.

But "my faith" is not something that can be forced on anyone nor can any amount of personal fervor, reasoning or argumentation convey this experience of God to another. According to Saint Paul, personal faith is a gift of God (Ephesians 2:8-9). And Jesus himself said it is the result of the working of the Spirit, who is like the wind, blowing where it will (John 3:7-8).

Thus, rather than fret and worry about whether someone experiences God the way I do, I simply pray that the Holy Spirit will have his way with them, whatever that way might be. Then I leave it with God because ultimately, it's his problem, not mine. Meanwhile, as I wait upon his Spirit to blow new life into the hearts of others, I show them the same love and respect I would like to be shown.

Mother Teresa cared for many sick and dying people regardless of their beliefs because when she looked into their faces she saw the face of Jesus. That, I believe should be a primary outward expression of "my faith," not coercing others to believe as I do, but rather my determining to see in others the face of Jesus.

Finally, the **eleventh dance step to joy is dance with life in the shadow of death!** Years ago I visited a mission church in Las Cruces, New Mexico, which met in a funeral home chapel. The pastor would place the pulpit in the alcove of the chapel where there would normally be a casket. From the ceiling soft pink and blue spotlights shone down on the pastor during services. I remember joking with him, "You look so natural under those lights." We both laughed.

But death isn't funny. I've had three members of my family killed by gun violence. Both my wife's parents died of cancer. So did my father. My mother died just over a year ago. My little grandson Mikey lost his battle with leukemia. I hate death! It never gets easy to lose a loved one; no matter how long you've had them, no matter how sick they've been. It never gets easy to face our own death. We tell jokes about death like I've just done to ease the pain a bit, but it doesn't really help. Preparation does.

That means having a good death plan. A well thought out death plan is a list of things that we need to accomplish before our last day arrives. It should include such things as completing a medical directive, writing a will with a preamble that speaks of one's faith, values, and hopes for one's family, distributing or disposing of personal items, making arrangements for our funeral or other type of service, stating our preference for what happens to our body, and seeing that our family is informed about all this. When you get them done these preparations can help you dance.

And so can faith. For me, that's both "The Faith," with a capital "F," and "my faith" with a small "f." Confessionally and personally, I am convinced in my heart of hearts that when the soul leaves the body it is taken by the angels to be with the Lord. There it is kept safe till the resurrection. When Jesus comes again, body and soul are reunited to live forever with him in a wonderful new world where there's no more sin or sorrow or suffering or death. That's my blessed hope. That's the solid floor I dance on.

Those who share this blessed hope can dance with life right now, even if the shadow of death is near. Martin Luther is supposed to have said, "Even if I knew that tomorrow the world would go to pieces, I would still plant my apple tree today." We don't know when we'll die, or a loved one, or when the world will end. But faith gives us hope to carry on today regardless of when those things come to pass.

Shortly before he died, my father-in-law Lonnie Beyer was on his tractor cutting hay. He continued to do the things he loved as long as God gave him life. That's the way it is for people of faith. They dance with life in the shadow of death.

In my view, heaven is not living forever on a cloud somewhere or spending eternity in church. It's doing useful things. So I'm thinking that if Lonnie left his hay on the ground in this life, after the resurrection he'll be baling it, and loving every minute of it. Believing this way leaves my heart dancing. I hope it does yours, too. Because *it's never too late to dance!*

www.ingramcontent.com/pod-product-compliance
Lightning Source LLC
Chambersburg PA
CBHW032103080426
42733CB00006B/402